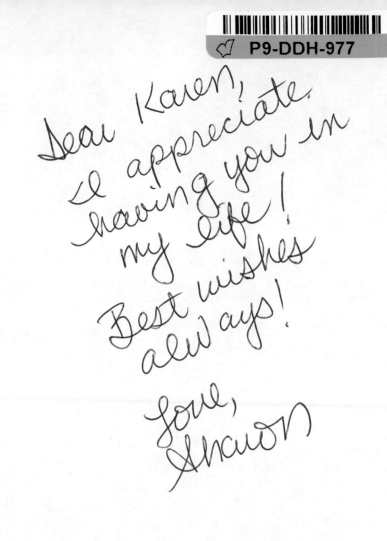

Dear Karen,
I appreciate
having you in
my life!
Best wishes
always!

Love,
Sharon

THE ART OF BLISSFUL
PARENTING

Teaching Your Children How To
Follow Their Internal Guidance

SHARON BALLANTINE

BALBOA.
PRESS

A DIVISION OF HAY HOUSE

Balboa Press books may be ordered through booksellers or by contacting:

Balboa Press
A Division of Hay House
1663 Liberty Drive
Bloomington, IN 47403
www.balboapress.com
1 (877) 407-4847

Because of the dynamic nature of the Internet, any web addresses or links contained in
this book may have changed since publication and may no longer be valid. The views
expressed in this work are solely those of the author and do not necessarily reflect the
views of the publisher, and the publisher hereby disclaims any responsibility for them.

The author of this book does not dispense medical advice or prescribe the use
of any technique as a form of treatment for physical, emotional, or medical
problems without the advice of a physician, either directly or indirectly. The
intent of the author is only to offer information of a general nature to help you
in your quest for emotional and spiritual well-being. In the event you use any
of the information in this book for yourself, which is your constitutional right,
the author and the publisher assume no responsibility for your actions.

Any people depicted in stock imagery provided by Thinkstock are models,
and such images are being used for illustrative purposes only.
Certain stock imagery © Thinkstock.

Print information available on the last page.

ISBN: 978-1-5043-4337-4 (sc)
ISBN: 978-1-5043-4339-8 (hc)
ISBN: 978-1-5043-4338-1 (e)

Library of Congress Control Number: 2015917224

Balboa Press rev. date: 11/24/2015

Contents

This book is dedicated to my loving children and husband, Brittany, Raven Dustin and Jay.

Introduction

Parenting is a lifelong commitment. While parenting can be a beautiful experience, not every moment is blissful. In *The Art of Blissful Parenting*, I offer you an expanded perspective of yourself, your child, and the most important job in the world: being a parent.

I want to show you how to have a more joyful connection with your child and a more stress-free parenting experience by accessing and following your Internal Guidance System. Your IGS informs you, through your feelings and intuition, which path will best serve you and make you happy. Familiarizing yourself with this powerful system will allow you not only to be in a more joyful state, but also to teach your child about his or her IGS—so that they can choose for themself the path that best serves them.

Throughout the book I provide practical tools as well as spiritual guidance that applies to children of all ages, including young adults. I have also integrated various personal stories that illustrate a range of parenting concerns.

Regardless of the challenges you may be facing as a parent, my hope is that *The Art of Blissful Parenting* will inspire you to create your own blissful experiences with those whom you cherish most dearly.

Warmly,

Sharon Ballantine

CHAPTER 1

Discovering My Internal Guidance System

I came into this world a happy, optimistic child. Growing up, my family life and experiences progressed from happy and fun to less so—not unlike many people's lives. Even as a child, I always had a clear sense of what I wanted and what felt good to me, whether it was a person, an experience, or a material object. And despite serious losses and hardships, things always seemed to work out for me. As I got older, I came to expect that I could manifest what I wanted.

As a child, I had no idea about the laws of the Universe and how they were responsible for my ability to consciously regulate my wellbeing. What I did know was this: I had always followed my feelings in order to avoid what I *didn't* want to experience and to experience what I *did* want. It was how I *felt* about something that determined the outcome for me, and I never questioned the validity of my feelings. I innately trusted that if a decision or course of action felt good, it was the right one for me.

Why did I trust my feelings? When I was young, I thought just because I wanted something, I should have it. My life experience showed me that if I followed what I would much later come to know as my Internal Guidance System, I could manifest what I wanted if I had positive feelings about my desire. Depending on what the desire consisted of, and my beliefs about it, I could want it and have it manifest quickly, or want something and then be inspired as to the best and right way to get it. I learned that negative emotion, while important in our evolution, is resistance. It temporarily blocks our access to Universal wellbeing and everything we want. My inclination to follow what felt positive and good to me was an intuitive way of avoiding resistance and tapping into my Internal Guidance System.

By the time I was a young adult, I started to study the Universal Law of Attraction and other spiritual modalities. It soon became clear to me how I was able to have a certain vision and then have it manifest, sometimes so quickly that it made my head spin. I realized through my studies that all my life I had been unknowingly working within the Universal Law of Attraction and following my Internal Guidance System.

WHAT IS THE LAW OF ATTRACTION?

This governing law of our Universe states that thought is a vibration/energy that goes out into the Universe as a signal, and what you will receive in return will always match this vibration. For example: a high vibration/energy is one of appreciation, love, gratitude, and positive expectation. A lower vibration is one of anger, doubt, fear, and so on. After several seconds of thinking a thought—whether it is something you want and that feels good, or something you don't want and feels bad, the Universe will send you what matches this signal formed by your thoughts. This will come to you in the form of "like" thoughts, people, and experiences. In other words, your manifestations.

The Law of Attraction also teaches that what you continually focus on becomes larger and is ultimately brought into what you experience. Through practice, I taught myself to think about and focus only on what I wanted to experience, at least most of the time. When I found myself starting down the path of thinking about what I did not want, which resulted in my feeling bad and manifesting unwanted experiences, I practiced my way to better-feeling thoughts—ones that opened up my possibilities and helped me feel better.

I learned that I was in control of my life because I could control the direction of my thoughts, which determined what I manifested. I realized that with practice and *intention* I could turn my negative emotion into positive emotion by deliberately making a choice as to what I was thinking—and therefore, feeling.

If this all sounds a bit hard to believe, I'd like to pinpoint specific events and moments in my life that illustrate how I came to recognize my Internal Guidance System at work. Growing up, I had no idea there was such a "system" at play—only that something unseen was working on my behalf.

PARENTING MYSELF

Growing up, I loved my parents very much. They both helped me become who I am today, not necessarily by overtly teaching me things but by providing me with the chance to witness what their lives were like. Although I always felt loved and supported by my mom, she was only able to be emotionally present to a certain extent. Even as a young child, I could see that she often felt melancholy, and I sensed that it was difficult for her when my dad was away, working in a foreign country. She worked full-time and was essentially raising two children as a single parent. She had little time to focus on herself, let alone invest in her interior self, engage in a spiritual practice, or teach one to me.

My dad got a job in Chile when I was four years old and moved us 6,000 miles from our comfortable home in the suburbs of Seattle. Our family lived in Chile until I was ten, when Mom brought my brother and me back to the US to continue our education. I thought it was strange that my father wasn't coming with us, but my parents assured my brother, Ken, and me that Dad would soon follow. It wasn't to be, and within two years my mom and dad were divorced. I was a preteen by then, busy with my life and activities. I remember missing my dad, and at times it was difficult because he wasn't present at school activities, holidays, and important celebrations. But it didn't feel terrible that he wasn't living with us day to day, because he was always available to me by phone, letters, and visits. As for my brother, he was a cheerful child, and the divorce didn't seem to affect him adversely at the time, as far as I could tell. We were kids and never spoke to each other about it.

Mom seemed to be in survival mode. She liked to drink wine in the evenings, which was when she shared many of her unhappy childhood memories with me, usually over a frozen TV dinner. She never mentioned Dad or the divorce, so I never knew if her sadness was related to that. As a teenager, I remember feeling bad for Mom. She had grown up in a dysfunctional household and felt powerless to improve her life. I knew that even though our own family did not live in perfect harmony every day, I didn't feel powerless myself, and I had learned that I was in control of not what happened to me, but my reaction to it. By witnessing Mom's lack of personal power, I either knew innately or decided at that time that that would never be me because I wanted to be happy in the long term as well as in the present moment.

Soon I was involved in dancing, baton twirling, and Girl Scouts, and it was at this point that I first started noticing how well things went for me when I was happy and having fun. I got what I wanted when I felt this way, and in this manner, I learned to manifest my own happiness. Over the years, I would actively learn to cultivate this feeling of happiness.

Most kids are masters at having fun. It is what they do. Having fun made me happy! Any kind of fun, such as being with my friends or doing an activity that I enjoyed. I think my gift as I matured was in identifying my quality of life when I was happy and having fun, versus my quality of life when I wasn't. Clearly, things didn't flow well and get me what I wanted when I felt bad and negative, but they sure did when I was feeling good. For example, if I wanted a certain something or a particular reaction from my mom, I realized that believing I would get it and focusing only on that outcome gave me a huge advantage, as opposed to being pessimistic or demanding toward her. I came to notice that my manifestations were a direct result of what I was thinking and expecting.

What I now know is that it is generally easy for kids to be joyful because they haven't yet learned to get in their own way. It comes naturally for most children to expect to receive what they want. Early on, I was able to notice the difference between positive and negative expectations and use that insight to my advantage.

I also discovered that, try as I might, I could not force situations to go my way. And let me make this perfectly clear: I am a person who likes things to go my way. I was somehow able to see that things flowed when I was happy and wasn't trying to force the issue, whereas things didn't go my way when I pushed against a situation over which I had no control. In those early years, I didn't know how to redirect my thoughts; that is, I didn't know how to feel better by choosing happier thoughts. I only noticed what I was manifesting based on how I was feeling.

After my parents' divorce, I had the chance to more closely witness my father's sense of optimism. He came to see us every year, and we would also visit him in Chile, which led to interesting adventures on the other side of the planet. Despite being a workaholic, Dad always felt joyful to me. He was always positive and had a passion for life that I could easily relate to. He took life's difficult situations in stride. He got up, dusted himself off, and moved forward smiling. Dad inspired me with his joyful outlook, and although he endured a number of very difficult physical problems during the last five years of his life, his attitude was always positive. Whenever he took my brother and me out to dinner, he provided us with life lessons along with whatever we chose from the menu. He coached us and gave us general advice about how to succeed in life. I don't recall his specific advice, but I remember gobbling it up like it was my last meal because it felt good to be with him and his words resonated with me.

I never thought it was a bad thing that Dad didn't live with us because we maintained our loving connection 6,000 miles away from each other. Without a live-in father figure, and with Mom busy trying to support our family, I had more freedom than most of my friends. In fact, I was horrified at their lack of freedom. Unlike me, they had to be home at a certain time and report their whereabouts. They were forced to answer to two parents, account for their actions, and follow fairly strict standards. The list of restrictions seemed endless.

In contrast, my teen years were spent in total blissful freedom, and since I was a good kid with good grades, that also worked in my favor. Don't get me wrong, I did check in at home and Mom knew where I was … most of the time. But growing up with such freedom laid the groundwork for being able to depend on myself for direction. I didn't have anyone telling me what I should do and when, so I got to choose for myself, making my own decisions. Again, how I felt about something when I considered doing it or having it determined my choices and experiences. And this sort of parenting myself helped me to learn to look within.

I believe that as we grow up, we consciously and subconsciously decide whom we want to be based on what we are experiencing. As a child, I was living some of what I wanted and some of what I didn't want. Witnessing those parts of my mother's life that didn't feel good to her helped me to clarify how I wanted to feel and live my own life. It didn't feel natural for me to be unhappy. So when I observed my mom's unhappiness, I wanted to support her but not share in those feelings. In contrast, my dad was a generally happy person who experienced hardships. I witnessed his decision to initially feel bad about his situation but to quickly find his way back to feeling good. I saw him do this by turning his focus away from his problems and continuing to make plans for his life—which, it was evident, he felt was a really good life.

MY BROTHER, KEN

In our childhood photographs, my brother, Ken, is bright-eyed and usually smiling or laughing. We were only a year and a half apart and had such fun growing up together. In our teen years, when I was out having fun and living life, Ken spent the majority of his time at home, even though he had no restrictions put on him by our mother. Freedom just wasn't as important to Ken as it was to me. He seemed content to be at home with his music, at school, at work, or sometimes with friends.

At about the time he entered puberty, I noticed a change in Ken. He was no longer a happy-go-lucky kid. He was a very accomplished young man, an A student, and he also possessed extraordinary talents. He played several different musical instruments, even though he couldn't read a note of music. I watched him as he listened to songs on the radio or on an album, then picked up one of his instruments—the drums, piano, or guitar—and in a matter of minutes was able to play the song. Ken was so gifted at piano that he was asked to accompany the singers at school. When he chose his music, it was often wild, jazzy songs that used every key on the keyboard. This routinely resulted in the school needing to have the pianos tuned, since Ken played on them with such passion!

The change in Ken seemed to be a sullenness that wasn't there in his childhood, a quiet introspection that none of us guessed was depression. He never did drugs or got in any trouble whatsoever. Although he wasn't very social, he had several good friends. It was during his mid-teens that Mom came to me one morning and said that Ken had confided in her that he had considered suicide.

Soon thereafter, Ken started seeing a psychologist, but I never noticed any marked improvement. Even after he had been going for a few years, he didn't seem any happier. To make matters worse, our mother had been battling a debilitating illness, and when Ken was twenty and I was twenty-one, she passed away. Since Mom and Ken were very close, I was worried about his emotional wellbeing. Dad flew up from Chile for my mother's funeral, and it was then that he asked Ken if he wanted to live in Chile with him. If he moved to Chile, Ken would be able to play his music and have a nice life. Ken declined Dad's offer, which surprised me.

At the time, Ken was going to a community college and had a full-time job in the office of a sports club. I think he chose to not live with our dad because he didn't feel as close to him as I did. So, our father returned to Chile. With his financial backing, Ken and I remodeled the upstairs of the small house we'd inherited from Mom. I had moved back home, having recently returned from spending a year in Chile with Dad, and the house felt so good and updated. But Ken didn't seem to find joy in the remodel, or anything else, for that matter.

As I had done many times over the past several years, I tried to talk to Ken about making the choice to be happy. I told him I felt happiness was a decision, and I gave him examples of how I saw and found joy in the little things in life. This was the best way I could explain at the time for how one can go about finding happiness, as I had no knowledge yet of how to explain our Internal Guidance System. I wanted to believe that my brother was able to make the choice to choose joy, but I came to see that maybe it was out of his control. During our conversations about happiness, he seemed to genuinely want to be happy, but he couldn't maintain the feeling for very long. I believe there were only certain things that made Ken happy, and music was one of them.

A year after Mom died, I married Mark, my high-school sweetheart, and we initially moved in with Ken, to the house he and I owned. Mark and I lived with Ken for four months. Then we got our own place. On the weekend when Mark and I moved to our new house, my brother killed himself.

We had come back to the old house to get a few last things and found a long letter from Ken on the kitchen table. It outlined what to do with all his things. I had already started to think that maybe Ken's depression had been out of his control. As often as I had tried to coach and support him, I never felt he was able to choose to move forward in a happier way.

The hardest, most heart-wrenching thing I have ever had to do was to call my dad in Chile and tell him his son was dead. The sorrow in my father's voice broke my heart all over again.

My mother and brother's deaths occurred within a year and a half of each other, and I found tremendous comfort in having my dad. I now felt absolutely sure that this meant that he would live for a very long time. I felt he simply had to because the rest of my family was gone. Sadly, that was not the case. Within the next year and a half, Dad would also die, at age fifty-one.

LOSS AND RENEWAL

A simple case of athlete's foot that had never healed and had gone undiagnosed resulted in my dad contracting an untreatable case of gangrene due to his ongoing circulatory disease. I was horrified to learn of Dad's prognosis and couldn't imagine what to expect. His leg had to be amputated, and after his surgery in the States, I went to live with him and his new wife Sylvia in Chile for a year, to be of support. I was twenty years old.

Dad settled into bed to continue his recovery, and I settled into my new environment for the next year. My father's life was now transformed. He would later be fitted for prosthesis so he could walk with crutches, and his car was retrofitted to be fully driven with his hands.

The next few months were a challenge for Dad, but he had a psychologist come to the house every week, which quickly resulted in excellent benefits. Not being one to feel sorry for himself, my father soon became the happy, positive person I knew and loved. He learned to move quite well with his crutches, which allowed him to attend the horse races where his Thoroughbreds ran. My life in Chile during this time was fun and happy, surrounded by a group of amazing friends that my stepmother Sylvia had introduced me to.

Dad had two more amputations—one on the leg that had already been operated on and finally on his other leg. Between operations, he and I traveled a bit, always on the hunt for the perfect prosthesis, none of which were comfortable. Prior to having his foot amputated, it was a constant source of pain for Dad. Ultimately, he became wheelchair–bound.

Four years after my father's ordeal began, he was in intensive care in New York City, hooked up to a dozen machines. Once he was stabilized, all of the tubes removed, and in his own hospital room, he and I had one of the most memorable talks we had ever had together.

He had a great sense of humor and made a comment about how he felt like the Messiah, having suffered an inordinate amount of pain over the previous four-plus years. He was trying to be funny. I held his hand as he lay there, and I said, "Dad, please remember, you have lived more life and had more adventures than most people ever get to live." I reminded him of the fact that I'd never seen him feel sorry for himself; instead, he was a support to others during his own ordeal. He seemed to agree with my revelation.

Dad's joy and passion for living was what I admired most in him, and I was relieved to see a renewed surge of life come through him as he called and reconnected with his friends and contacts in Chile from his hospital bed in New York. That evening, I felt that all was well for the moment and decided to take a break from the hospital. The next morning, while I was dressing to go see Dad, the hospital called. They broke the news to me that he had passed away during the night. He was only fifty-one.

My father was cremated in New York, and the family and I had a small memorial service. I took his ashes with me as I headed back across the country to the west coast, where my husband Mark was waiting at home for me. I realized then that my life was altered forever. I had lost my beloved father, the last member of my immediate family.

It seemed impossible to me that I had lost my whole family, my mom, dad, and brother, within three years. The odds of this actually happening seemed astronomical.

I was, however, very clear about one thing: I had somehow been spared the feeling of complete devastation after finding myself without my immediate family. I had been close to each of them, and we loved one another dearly. I missed them so much, and I went through what I believe was a normal grieving process for each one of them. Yet, instead of feeling completely ruined by the loss, I felt driven toward a spiritual quest. Given the circumstances, I believed there must have been a higher reason for their deaths in such a short period of time, and I decided to find some answers.

All of the experiences I had by the age of twenty-four helped me to question and then begin to define the kind of life I wanted to live, how I wanted to "see" myself—and what kind of parent I wanted to be when the time came. My spiritual path and the studies that I embarked upon after my family died gave me the direction and tools that I needed in order to accomplish the enlightenment I sought.

INITIATING MY SPIRITUAL STUDIES

My family was gone. Now what? I was almost twenty-five years old, and life would never be the same. Technically, I would never have to work again since I had inherited millions of dollars from Dad, and there was no debt. But who would I be as I moved into the future with this new lifestyle? I had worked since I was sixteen years old, felt very independent, had been married less than two years, and didn't yet have children. After serious contemplation and introspection about who I was and where I thought I might be going, I decided it was time to reinvent myself, my inner self.

I remember actively thinking that this reinvention would have to be thorough. So I asked myself: Did I like who I was? Would I take the person I currently was with me into my future? The answer shocked me: *no*. But why not? And how would I go about changing myself?

I had always been keenly aware of my Internal Guidance_System, although I didn't have a name for it yet, as I was accustomed to looking internally for my answers. I had always been guided by how things felt in my heart as opposed to using my head and overthinking. I knew that my behavior toward others did not always feel good to me, so I wanted to create a transformation, but I wasn't completely sure how to go about it. I did know that any changes I made would have to be done with a loving, patient attitude toward myself, as this would be an ongoing, long-term process.

Memories of past interactions with my family, friends, and coworkers came flooding through me. I recalled how sometimes I was keenly aware of who I was becoming and choosing to be, yet at other times I was not choosing consciously, and this didn't feel good. Moving forward, I wanted to feel more present and in the moment with the people I was with, and I wanted to be more aware of others' feelings and desires. **In the big picture, I wanted to feel that I was of value to those around me and to the world, and live without judgment.** I saw myself living my highest ideals, my best life, and this felt amazing to visualize, internalize, and intend.

To start this process, I first had to be aware and conscious of where I wanted to go and who I wanted to be. I had a very clear vision of being a person who feels good about my treatment of and interaction with others. Next came the intention of change, of choosing a new way of being. But what did that mean?

Intention is a powerful statement to the Universe. It is what propels us forward, and I knew it didn't have to be complicated. The intention I stated was that I would, in every conscious moment, be the best person I could be toward myself and others. How I felt as I interacted with others would show me if I was heading in my desired direction. I would be in alignment with my intention if I felt good during these interactions.

To reinvent my inner and outer world, I first had to be able to take a good look at myself and be able to have an honest interior dialogue. These are the things I focused on:

- Being conscious of my exterior self—how I am toward others.
- Knowing my belief system. Examining my beliefs and letting go of limiting beliefs that didn't serve me, such as judgment toward others.

- Trusting in myself, my ability to change and create the highest and best vision of myself.

- Affirming my faith in the Universe and that it is always guiding me.

- Holding steady the intention of my willingness to change, even when it becomes challenging.

- Reinforcing my capacity to listen to my heart—my Internal Guidance System, as I would later learn to call it.

- Fine-tuning my ability to continually focus forward toward my future, not my past.

- Being strong in my willingness to change my story (what I say to others and to myself) from what I'm currently experiencing to what I *want* to be experiencing.

So my quest began. I wanted tools to help me, and I wanted to read books from which I could learn. I asked the Universe for help with all of this. Gone were the romance novels that I had spent my twenties reading. Instead, I sought books that could offer me spiritual guidance. I have never been religious, and my parents never taught us any formal religion. I don't even remember how I learned about God, but I had God in my life and felt a strong connection to a higher power. My faith was strong.

I visited one of my favorite bookstores to start my quest. As I searched through the hundreds of books dealing with spiritual studies, I felt overwhelmed. How would I know which book was right for me? In the years that followed, I would make many such trips to numerous bookstores. Over time, I learned to relax, manifest the book that was for my highest good, and trust completely in what I pulled off the shelf. I would sometimes close my eyes and reach out, knowing that the book I touched would be the right one.

Among the first spiritual books I read were several written by Shirley MacLaine, in which she shared her personal and spiritual quest. I loved her sense of humor and how she received messages from the energetic world. I was in awe of the magic she lived and I knew we could all create.

I also read James Redfield. His stories of self-discovery incorporated fantasy and fun, and I learned to expand my perceptions.

One of the series of books that would become the basis of what helped me learn to create my world, and what I would later teach to my children, were the *Conversations with God* books by Neale Donald Walsch. Neale's talks with God about every subject, the laws of the Universe, and the ways we create our world spoke deeply to my inner source and guidance. I have read all of his books, several times each.

As the laws of the Universe were discussed, I wanted to learn more about them, mainly the Universal Law of Attraction, which says that what you think about, you attract into what you experience as your manifestations, whether they are wanted or not. Fascinating! As a result, I later came upon Esther and Jerry Hicks and their many books, CDs, and DVDs. They offered a complete and comprehensive study of the Law of Attraction taught by the consciousness of what they called Abraham, who was channeled through Esther Hicks. They focused only on the Law of Attraction and wrote about being in alignment with the Source and tapping into the wellbeing that is the Universe. Their teachings felt amazing to me.

In these teachings, the Hickses presented the concept of one's own Internal Guidance System. They explained that how we feel is in direct correlation with, and an indicator of, how connected we are with the Source—Source being our higher self, God, the greater part of us that is our connection to the Universe or energetic world. I was finally able to define the process in my life with terminology that referred to it as the Internal Guidance System. Through the Hickses' books, I learned more about vibration, focus, and intention, and their teachings became a mirror of my life and how I moved through it. I was given a new and valuable vocabulary. I also learned in great detail how to be a deliberate creator and consciously choose the life I wanted. These teachings were a Godsend to me—literally.

As the years passed and I studied more of Esther and Jerry Hicks' material, it became a rudimentary foundation from which I later taught my kids while creating a basis for them to follow their own Internal Guidance System.

INSPIRATION FROM ANGELS

Another area of my studies revolved around the role of angels in our lives. We are always guided and helped by the angels. We can tap into this guidance by listening and feeling the sometimes quiet, sometimes bold messages that we receive in various forms.

Growing up, I had heard of and read stories about people who received messages from angels. I always thought these people must be special, and I wanted to feel special, too. I learned that one of the ways angels work with people is through number sequences. I came to know, for example, that 444 meant many angels were with you and that all was well.

I had read that all you have to do is ask for guidance, and that is exactly what I did. First, I set the intention of having a relationship with my angels, asserting that I was willing to ask for and receive their help. I was then guided to buy a book on angel numbers and their meanings. My initial experience: I was reading the book about angel numbers. I put down my book, closed my eyes, and asked to be guided in whatever manner I could understand best. My life has never been the same since.

The number sequences started to come to me, and I saw them everywhere: on billboards, car license plates, television, and so on.

I realized that the numbers came as a spontaneous, unexpected gift. One of the most memorable experiences came to me when I was driving on a back-country road near our home. I rarely saw another car on this particular road, so I was surprised when a car suddenly passed me going slowly in the opposite direction. I happened to notice that the license plate included the numbers 044. Then another car followed behind it with the numbers 404. To top it off, another car came immediately behind it, and the plate included the numbers 400. By then I knew I was being spoken to through these similar numbers. I couldn't wait to get home and look up the numbers in my angel book. Once I read their meaning, I felt so much appreciation. This particular book described that any sequence of zeroes and fours means that the angels are with you, surrounding you with their divine love, bliss, and protection.

Through the years, the number sequences occurred so many times that I grew completely confident of their importance. These days, I also use the numbers book by holding it to my heart, closing my eyes, and asking that I receive the number that is right for me that day. Each number has its own clear and loving message.

Being conscious of everything that comes into your experience is an important first step in recognizing your messages, which may come as a chance meeting of someone new or an old acquaintance, the dialogue in a movie, or a conversation with a person that rings true and inspires you toward something you want or toward an answer you've been seeking. You will always be sent the answers you have requested. So, intend on being in a state of gently noticing everything in your world because it all has meaning for you.

As the emerging new "me" was being created through my studies, personal work, and spiritual practice, I came to realize many things. I was able to truly see and know that we all have the ability to choose and create our reality by focusing on our desires rather than on the unwanted things in our lives. I came to know that I could be my best self by choosing to be. Prior to my studies, I didn't know that we are all in control of our emotions, thoughts, and actions. I had previously believed that we were the victims of our emotions. I never realized that we could control the direction of our thoughts and thus, ultimately, our emotions.

Of course we all experience negative emotions. But we also have the ability to change our thoughts to ones that feel better and lead to a better-feeling emotion—a more positive emotion.

I also learned that we can choose our responses by not being reactive to unwanted experiences and people in our lives. And I came to the realization that the Universe is always on my side, guiding me toward what I want and my highest choices.

I completely transformed my life and experience when I came to know these truths. I learned to consciously listen to my own Internal Guidance System by paying attention to how I felt. When I thought about a desire, an idea, choice, or anything in my life, I focused on how it felt. If it felt good when I thought about it, I knew I was in alignment with it, and it would be right for me. If it felt bad, frightening, or had any negative emotion attached to it, regardless of my desire for it, I knew I was not in alignment with it. I would have to get into alignment with the thought or idea before it could serve me and be right for me. If I couldn't do this, it wouldn't be a wise decision for me to take any action.

What does it mean to be in alignment? It means you're offering one vibration/energy to the Universe. Alignment is when you have a desire with no thoughts that contradict it. This means you aren't sabotaging what you want with negative thoughts, which split your energy. An example would be: You want a new job but tell yourself you aren't qualified for it, don't deserve it, or have any other thought or belief about it that doesn't feel good. This means you aren't in alignment with what you want. If, on the other hand, you have a desire that you believe you deserve, can have, and believe it will come to you, then you are in alignment with what you want. It means you're thinking the same thought as your Source (or higher self). Your Source will only ever think the highest thought possible, and it will believe in all of the possibilities available. This is a part of you. When your energy is not split, you'll feel good and thus be *in alignment*. You must be in alignment with what you want in order for it to manifest.

DISCOVERING YOUR INTERNAL GUIDANCE SYSTEM

Now that you have a sense of how I discovered and came to rely on my Internal Guidance System, I invite you to discover yours. I firmly believe that when you do, you will be better prepared to guide and support your children as they become the vibrant, joyful, self-reliant individuals they were meant to be.

NOTES

CHAPTER 2

Befriending Your Internal Guidance System

I n this chapter, I will introduce you to some of the core principles that you will use to guide your children. In order to teach them, you must first embody these principles and teach yourself how to use your own Internal Guidance System. Knowing how to be *in alignment* and how to return to being in alignment when confronted with stressful circumstances is key to being a supportive parent, as well as ensuring your overall wellbeing. I have included guidance in this area, as well. I now invite you to become acquainted with your Internal Guidance System.

THE PART OF YOU THAT KNOWS YOUR HIGHEST PATH

We all have an Internal Guidance System, although not everyone knows that they do and some ignore theirs. What is an IGS? It is the part of you that knows your highest path, your highest choice. It helps direct you to create what you came into this life to create.

Some people refer to it as their "gut" talking to them. Others say they are following their "heart."

Your IGS will never fail you. Will it help you make decisions for others? No. It's your own personal system that exists for you and only you. It speaks to you in the language of feelings, desires, and inspirations, *not* questions or pros and cons, which are generated from your head.

I have always felt my IGS intently from my heart. I never think about what decisions I will make. Instead, I feel my way through them. In fact, I believe you "feel" from your heart, never from your head. Your head is the rational, practical part of you. It will serve you well when it comes time to follow through with the inspired actions that your IGS has informed you are the right actions to take.

A powerful consequence of *not* following your IGS can manifest as a life full of regrets. Perhaps you wish that you had followed through on a certain action, rather than ignoring what your internal voice was trying to tell you. Or maybe you hear your Internal Guidance System speaking to you, but you don't trust its valuable guidance. Trust and faith in yourself and the Universe is an integral part of creating your divine life.

So how do you use your IGS? It sounds simple, and it can be, but it requires practice. You use your IGS by being aware of your feelings. When you are faced with a decision, ask yourself: How does it feel when I consider one option versus another? Be aware of those feelings; stop and pay close attention. Does it feel like your heart wants to propel you forward? Do you have a desire to move ahead with this choice? Do inspirational thoughts and ideas come through? Does it feel like there is no other option and that this choice is the only one for you? Or does it feel heavy or negative in your heart? Does it feel like you *should* do it rather than that you *want* to do it? This is your Internal Guidance System communicating with you.

The more you become conscious and aware of using your IGS, the easier it becomes to use it and to trust it. It will never fail you and will always direct you to your highest choice.

CHOOSING WHAT YOU DWELL ON

Most of us don't realize that we can control the *direction* of our thoughts. This means that as they start to make us feel bad, for example, we can choose instead to think about a subject we already know makes us happy. So, as we become more practiced in paying attention to which direction our thoughts are headed in, we can choose which course to take more quickly. Our choice is this: Do we continue with the thoughts that have started to make us feel bad, or do we decide to choose thoughts that make us feel better? We can apply this process to any issue, circumstance, or person in our lives.

What about when we don't have access to any real information to help guide our thoughts, and no apparent and obvious truth to get us started with a train of thought? When I say "have access," I mean that we don't have knowledge of or can't find additional information regarding a subject that we are thinking about.

For example, you may care about someone, but you don't have access to whether they care about you. Based on what you may have experienced of them, your practiced thought will start creating a belief. Any thought pattern practiced over and over will create a belief within you, which is why it is so crucial to make sure that the thought you are perpetuating is what you *want to believe*. In this particular example, you have a choice of two different trains of thought. The first train of thought includes all of the reasons why someone may not care about you; the second includes all the reasons why they probably do care about you. You may never have access to what is really true or going on with the person you care about, but you do get to choose *what you dwell on* and what you believe.

As you choose thoughts that result in self-pity and erode your self-esteem, you are *in resistance*, which means you are blocking off your wellbeing, your connection to the Universe. Consequentially, you will then be attracting what you don't want. And, as an added measure, you'll feel awful.

What if, on the other hand, you choose the higher path of thinking—those thoughts that lift your self-esteem as you are dwelling on all the positive attributes that are *you?* When we deliberately choose thoughts that cause us to feel better, and ultimately good, we release our resistance to our wellbeing. We now have the access we want to manifest our desires.

I have taught myself to do this very effectively through continual practice. It is a decision, every time, about what we dwell on. Make your "dwelling time" feel good by consciously observing the direction your thoughts are taking you and listening to the invented scenarios in your head. Do you like the story? If not, make up a new story. Take what you like about yourself, what you have to offer the world, and paint a beautiful picture. Each one of us comes into this life worthy of doing and creating the highest vision of ourselves. It is up to you to maintain this vision.

What you focus and dwell on is what you bring forward, what you create more of. Feeling good will always be your desired result. Being happy is the starting place where all of your magical creations come from.

THE LAW OF ATTRACTION

To review the Law of Attraction, this law helps you deliberately move through your life by changing unwanted habits of thought, limiting beliefs, and consciously choosing what you want to focus on. It does this by responding to the energy of what you are focusing on and giving you your manifestations. The Law of Attraction is the law that governs our Universe; it is absolute and universal, which means it applies to everyone at all times. I liken it to the law of gravity, in that the LOA works in every moment and requires no attention or action from us to function. It is, however, much more fun to be a *deliberate* creator than a creator by default.

You have the choice either to let life happen to you or to tap into the universal flow and deliberately create your life and everything in it. You get to script it because *you are the creator of what you experience.*

Intention is everything! Our intent is what propels us forward, and it is our strongest ally. Always being aware of and clear about what you intend to bring into your life will help you create it. There is only wellbeing that flows toward you and through you from the Universe, and although the flow can't be stopped, it can be blocked off. As I mentioned before, feeling bad blocks off access to what you want and all of your wellbeing. Positive emotion releases your resistance and gives you back your wellbeing. For this reason, caring about how you feel is the most important thing in your life. How you're feeling is the gauge telling you in which direction you're headed: toward what you want or away from it.

As human beings, we are vibrational energy, and our thoughts go out to the Universe as a vibrational frequency. What you attract into your life experience is whatever matches this vibration. Your manifestations will come back to you in like thoughts, people, and experiences. What you give your attention to expands and is brought into your experience in the form of things that you want and things that you don't want. Deliberately creating your life begins with imagining and training yourself to focus your attention on what you want, and being specific about the details of your desires.

In order to create what you truly want, you have to *feel* it first. Ask yourself: What will it *feel* like to have this wanted thing, person, or experience? How does it feel to already own it, touch it, experience it? Think also about what you want and *why* you want it. The *why* helps to further clarify your desire by acknowledging the aspects of what you want and how you want to feel by having your desire manifested. What is the *essence* of this desire—the basic, real, and invariable nature of it? To manifest what you want, you must be in *vibrational alignment* with that desire. In other words, your thoughts and actions must support what you have said you want. Your thoughts and actions must not be in conflict or resistance; they must be in sync.

When your thoughts and actions regarding your desires are in vibrational alignment, it means you are making choices while connected to Source energy. Source refers to God, the Universe— the all-knowing, wise part of you that has the Big Picture vision of your life. When you are connected to the Source, you feel joyful, enthusiastic, eager, energized, and satisfied. Life flows more freely, and you're offering no resistance. You allow the *wanted* things, people, and experiences to come into your life by staying out of your own way. When you aren't connected to the Source, your negative emotions and feelings block off your wellbeing and all the things you want.

Your Internal Guidance System is the indicator that shows you if you are moving toward what you want or away from it. This information comes to you through your emotions. Again, it's important to remember that *what you focus on gets bigger and is manifested*. If you focus on what is lacking in your situation, you will only attract more deficiencies, whereas if you focus on what you want, you'll have an easier time manifesting it.

How does this process work? Let's say that you want more financial abundance. You first have to *feel abundant* in other ways not related to money before the Universe can give you more financial abundance. It's the feeling that counts not the subject. You want to amp up feeling abundant. One way you can amp up feeling abundant is by appreciating all the ways in which you already have abundance in your life. You may have an abundance of friends, business contacts, or health. Remember to take the time to connect with your feelings about what you want, rather than focusing on your thoughts about it. Another crucial aspect of this process is to *make peace with the situation that you want to change.* If you continue to be frustrated about your given situation, you will hold yourself there. You can make peace by looking for and then feeling the positive aspects of your present condition—and lastly appreciating those things, however small they may be. You then must *practice being in appreciation.* Remember that the Universe will give you what you are thinking and focusing on.

Appreciation is an extremely high vibration/energy that will help you move out of resisting your current status and into the allowing of your desires to manifest. Sometimes you may find only a minute detail to appreciate. My advice is to dwell on this small aspect until it feels big. The Universe responds to what you're feeling, not the size of the desire or the aspect of whatever you are appreciating. Another way to make peace with your current circumstances is to fully surrender to the Universe, knowing that what you want, or the essence of it, is on its way to you. When you have surrendered, your energy is full of trust and faith—free of resistance and no longer attached to an end result. Surrender is not the same as giving up.

How do you know that what you want is there for you and waiting for you to allow it to come into your life? Where do desires go when you propel them out into the Universe? When a desire, either conscious or unconscious, is sent from you, it's released as energy and becomes a part of a *vibrational place* where all the desires you have ever had are held for you. It is yours alone; no one has access to it except you. It is from here that you call forth or allow what you have asked for to come from the *energetic world* into our physical world.

Think about your desires and nurture them with love and anticipation. Know they are there for you. As you remain focused on your desires, without all the negative emotion (also known as resistance), you'll have access to the information from the Universe that will help you allow your manifestations. The information will come to you in inspiration and impulses—those thoughts that drive us to take immediate action, all in the perfect time. This is referred to as *divine timing*.

How do we come to know what we want? Some desires are very clear, and some aren't. We may know we aren't fulfilled, but we may lack clarity regarding which direction we want to go. Out of our negative emotions—which show us what we don't want—comes our clarity about what we do want. Knowing what we don't want is the starting point from which we make a new choice, which is why we should consider our negative emotions a gift. We just don't want to dwell on negative emotions any longer than necessary to make a new choice. When we do the emotional work to get back to positive emotion (happiness), we can then allow ourselves to create what we want.

As you practice, practice, practice getting back as quickly as possible to feeling good, your happiness becomes more of an integrated part of your vibration and who you are. This means you will, in time, be more naturally happy. You'll more quickly default to happy because it has become your practice to feel this way. What you think about and feel becomes a part of your energy field and becomes an integral part of you as you practice this over time.

Notice when you are feeling happy, energetic, and inspired. Deliberately amp it up! This means prolonging the good thoughts you're thinking, the good feelings you're having from an experience, or even reliving a wonderful feeling memory from the past. The more time and energy you put into feeling good, the more access you have to creating magic in your life. Learn to be a positive thinker by refocusing your thoughts when you notice a train of thought that doesn't feel good. Change your reality by imagining all the possibilities.

Examine the beliefs and expectations you have for your life and ask yourself if you believe that all things are possible for you—because they are. Do you expect that what you ask for can come to you? It can. To achieve this, you must learn to speak to yourself in a way that supports your desires. Let negative self-talk fall away, and start telling yourself and others stories about yourself and where you're going that feel good. You will come to believe whatever you frequently talk about. Talk only about what feels good—whether it is about yourself or any other subject.

Does this mean that you can never have a conversation with someone about what is bothering you or bothering them? The answer is yes and no. Let me explain. Most of us want to be a support for others in our lives and feel like we are supported by them as well. But know this. We are of no use to anyone when we are in a lowered vibration, or when we feel bad. This is because the most powerful thing we will ever offer another person is our high vibration, our joy, which they may be inspired to rise to. When our high vibration, which may occur on a conscious or unconscious level, inspires others, it can change their lives.

So, how can we listen to our loved ones' tales of woe and actually be of help? We do this by listening to them without joining them in feeling bad. Our objective is to help them feel better, release their resistance, and have access again to their wellbeing. We can only do this when *we* are feeling good. This can absolutely be done, but it takes some practice. Most people believe they are of help when they join others in their misery, but this is a limiting belief.

What about when you want to vent and complain and tell someone about what you're feeling bad about? My first instinct is to say *don't do it*—but I'll elaborate. My own experience is this: When I talk about something I don't want or something that went wrong in my life, I feel bad. Feeling bad limits me, as I no longer have access to what I want. Since I don't like to feel bad, I have learned to limit this behavior. When I'm looking for help with a particular issue, I ask those I love for help and support in finding a solution. And solutions can't be found when we're feeling bad and focusing on the problem. I believe that venting and complaining are an entirely different matter and only result in perpetuating bad feelings. To vent and complain is rarely done to find solutions. On the other hand, when you live in a deliberate manner and choose a more positive focus, you become the cause of a better experience, consciously and deliberately.

INSPIRING: CHANGING OTHERS WITH YOUR VIBRATION AND EXPECTATION

Have you ever tried to change someone? I certainly have. It seems to be human nature to want to change another person's behavior so that we can feel better, safer, more secure, and ultimately happier. The reasons are endless. Yet, trying to change others doesn't always go as we planned. Our assumption is that others will want to change in order to please us, perhaps because they love us.

Occasionally other people will change for us. It does happen. If the change is consistent with that person's nature, it will be a positive feeling situation for everyone. However, if the request for change is unwelcomed or compromises whom the person really is, the requested change will be met with resistance. Why?

The reason is simple. It's because all of us are here on our own unique path with special reasons for what we have come to create in this lifetime. Each of us possesses an Internal Guidance System that leads us to our own personal highest truth and life mission. We don't come into this life to please others, and they don't come here to please us. Although it's nice when it happens, we can't always count on others to please us. Each of us is in charge of our own reality and happiness.

We may have spent years trying to change our spouses, children, family, and friends, to no avail. And yet, each of us possesses the one thing that will inspire and possibly even change others: our vibration, the energetic force that we emit with our thoughts and feelings. It is our vibration that other people respond to and give us more of whatever we have sent their way. This is constant, and you know this to be true, even if you have never noticed it.

People will always mirror back to you what you're feeling and, in turn, vibrate in your energy. If there's someone whom you have positive feelings about and you hold this positive vision while you're with them, as well as when they aren't in your presence, you will most often elicit a positive response from them. On the other hand, if you are with someone and are thinking about how you would like them to be different and how they are not measuring up to your expectations, then their deficiencies are what you will experience. In other words, you'll experience the unwanted behavior you expect or maybe even dread. Others will always give you the experience based on whatever you are expecting or believing about them. This is simply the Law of Attraction at work. You will always get what you expect and believe, no matter the circumstance.

So how do we get what we want? How do we elicit the behavior from others that we desire? How do we inspire others to be as we envision them?

We do this by holding steadfast in our thoughts the highest vision of that person, and we practice this until that is how we truly see them. What we practice with our thoughts is what will eventually become our truth. The way we think about others is how we will consistently experience them. Is your spouse or child irritating you? If you consistently see them as an irritant, you will experience them in this way on a regular basis. Not only is this process not very productive, it will never get us the desired behavior we keep saying we want.

Granted, when we're observing someone and they are showing us behaviors we don't want, it can be challenging to switch our focus to a vision of them that feels more positive. Initially, it may be easier to practice this new way of thinking and feeling about particular individuals when you aren't in their presence. Remember, a practiced thought will become what you believe over time.

Here is an example of how you might start this process:

- First, make feeling good your top priority. Do an activity you love. Fantasize your way to your happiness, or an anticipated fun event. Whatever thoughts lead you to feel good.

- Next, focus on the person in your life that you'd like to experience in a different, better-feeling way. See them in your mind's eye, and feel them being the highest vision you can have of them. Hold that thought as long as you can, and as long as it feels good. If it stops feeling good, the thought is no longer productive. Get back to feeling good about a different subject and try again later.

- Now, see and feel this person being the way you'd like. For instance: your spouse or significant other being more loving, your child putting more effort into his schoolwork, a coworker being more dependable, your boss being more respectful, or your best friend being kinder. You may even envision everyone in the world being more at peace. Experience how good it feels to have the people in your life—and everyone throughout the world—achieve and be who they really are, their highest selves.

Whenever you think about this person, or are with them face-to-face, practice this new thought as often as you can. This will become integrated into what you experience as time goes on. Once you practice this enough and you're able to maintain this focus regarding this person, you'll experience what you've practiced.

We all want to improve our relationships in some way. There is no improvement too small or too large to manifest, because we're capable of manifesting whatever we want. Such positive changes are always based upon what we have come to expect from others and the world. What we believe we deserve will also make the difference in what we experience. Our job is to change our vision and our expectations and switch our limiting beliefs to *knowing* that everything is possible for us.

You can leave behind the years of practiced thought that only brought you more of what you didn't want in a particular relationship. Start with one person and practice your way to a new experience, an experience of attracting what you desire. This doesn't mean that things will change instantaneously, but it doesn't take long.

What you're thinking/feeling is more powerful than any action you can take, and you'll inspire others by living with inner joy, tranquility, and stillness. Notice how you feel when you're with positive, happy people. Chances are you feel good and are inspired by them. Likewise, others will be inspired to rise to your positive energy, to your highest vision of them and the world, and you'll see a change in how others respond to you and act around you. They will feel better about themselves, and you will have a more positive experience of them.

REMEMBER WHO IS IN CONTROL OF YOUR EXPERIENCE

There are times when we immerse ourselves in our daily routine—it's often referred to as our *present reality*—and forget the bigger picture. During these moments, we sometimes give our power to others. Our power is given to others when we let them determine if we are happy or not, given their behavior. This is why it is important to remember who is in control of your experience at all times: you are, not others. When we buy into the illusion that others control our experience and manifestations, we're left feeling powerless. And it's important to remember that we can't create what we want from feeling powerless.

At one point or another, we have all given our power to others. We may have given our power to our bosses and let them determine what we experience in our jobs based on their behavior or expectations. Our lovers and spouses are gifted our power when we allow our happiness to be determined by their treatment of us or by whatever mood they are in.

We also turn over our power to our children. The quality of our day and the joy we allow ourselves to experience can be determined by whether their behavior has measured up to our expectations or how loving they are toward us.

We've also become experts at giving our power to people we don't even know. The grocery clerk, a receptionist, or the individual who cuts us off on the road—the list is endless. Other people have power over us when we are *reactive*, which often means we are experiencing negative emotion/feelings. In other words, we give others our power when we allow them to take us away from our happiness.

The laws of the Universe are absolute, and they include the fact that no one can create our experience. Each person creates their own experience by reacting to what is in their *present reality* and by what they believe and expect in any given situation.

We all possess a tendency to be reactive, meaning a knee-jerk reaction that is spontaneous and not deliberate. When things are going well and we are having a pleasant experience, it makes sense to react with joy, positive expectation, a sense of fun, and other positive emotions. If, however, what we're confronted with is not what we want, then being reactive will likely manifest as a negative emotion. We'll feel bad, and we won't get what we want.

I recently had a revelation—an "aha" moment—regarding the true power of how this works. I found myself in a situation where I wanted a certain outcome. After several days of trying to force my desired result, it finally became clear to me: I had given my power to another person because I wanted a response from them that would give me what I wanted. I couldn't control the outcome, and I was letting my happiness depend on it. I was bucking the Universe, and it was not responding to me in the way that I wanted it to. You can't force and push against anything to get a desired result. You must allow it to come to you.

It's only from feeling happiness, which results in a high vibration, that you are able to inspire others to meet your desires. Unfortunately, at that time, I wasn't able to inspire anyone with my vibration. I was feeling angst and frustration. And yet, even in the midst of my temporary meltdown, I experienced a quiet moment that felt like a divine inspiration. It was then that I found my focus and loudly declared to myself, "I am in control of my experience and what I manifest. No one else is." I had been expecting someone else to make this happen for me, and yet the moment I realized that such a thing wasn't possible, I took my power back. The message to myself was clear: Surrender to *what is* and feel that I am at peace with whatever the situation is now. When you do this, you allow the Universe to give you what you want because you are no longer resisting. Again, pushing against any situation won't give you what you want.

In the above example, I felt such a relief, as we often do after we get out of our own way! After a deep sigh, I felt my body completely relax. I remembered that I have faith that life works out for me and the outcome is always for my highest good, even if that outcome looks different than the scenario I had planned or pictured in my mind.

So I said to the Universe, "It doesn't look like this situation is going to match my vision. I surrender to what is, and it's okay. I am at peace with this, and I know all is well. This situation will resolve itself." Then I let it go. Consciously and deliberately, I envisioned releasing this situation up and out of my body to the Universe. *Thy will be done.*

I felt amazing. I then turned my focus to something random that made me feel good and started looking forward to my day. Once I did this, I knew I had released all my resistance. I was no longer trying to force things and push against them, and at that very moment I knew that somehow things would work out.

I didn't have to wait long. Within a short time, that very same day, the Universe gave me my miracle. The scenario I was placed in looked different than what I had previously pictured and wanted. Although the players were the same, I received a better-feeling experience than I could have imagined possible. It was incredible.

What I learned was this: I can only manifest what I want when I have released my resistance, which is negative emotion. The moment I released my resistance, I allowed what I wanted to come to me, fully and joyfully.

PRACTICING YOUR WAY TO HAPPINESS

Every emotion has a place on the *emotional ladder*. At the bottom of the ladder are powerlessness, grief, depression, despair, and fear. At the top of the scale are joy, appreciation, freedom, and love. All other emotions fall somewhere between the top and bottom of this ladder, which serves as a guide in determining where you currently are emotionally and where you would like to be.

In order for us to be an inspiration to our children or anyone else, we must use whatever tools we have on hand to practice returning to feeling good when "life happens" and we find ourselves less than joyful. There are many ways to do this, and I have included below two processes and an exercise that will help you to initiate this ongoing practice.

Two Helpful Processes

There are twenty-two processes identified by Law of Attraction teachers Jerry and Esther Hicks in the book *Ask and It Is Given*. I have chosen to include two of the processes that I start with when teaching others how to change their patterns of thought, belief, and expectation. You can use these processes as you learn how to redirect your thoughts.

1. Pivoting

For those who are first starting to practice this new way of being, I recommend the process of *pivoting*. This process shows you how to start noticing the direction your thoughts are going in and how to deliberately make a new choice.

Visualize a soldier marching in a straight line. This represents you going in a certain direction with your thoughts. When these thoughts don't feel good, *stop* and visualize this soldier pivoting and going in a different direction—the direction of choosing a thought that feels better. For example: You start to think about a coworker who has been annoying you, and you begin to feel angry. You've had this thought before, and you know what it does to your emotional state. You are now experiencing more awareness and consciously creating your life, so you gently stop this train of thought—perhaps by simply saying to yourself, "Stop."

Now deliberately choose a new direction of thought that feels better. You can start an appreciation process toward your coworker or turning your focus toward an activity that you enjoy. If you can't find anything good to think about toward this coworker at the moment, then a different train of thought will feel better. The objective is to *change your focus*. In this way, you deliberately change the direction of your thoughts away from ones that don't feel good and toward those that feel better. This process will help you become aware, conscious, and deliberate about going in a new direction toward what you want when your thoughts are taking you in the opposite direction.

2. *Wouldn't it be nice?*

Consider an upcoming experience or life event. You have no information as to how it will turn out, but you need assistance in keeping the highest possibilities open and your vibration in a high place so that you can manifest what you want. Perhaps you are going on a job interview and want to establish an optimistic, good-feeling attitude. You may start the process by telling yourself:

"Wouldn't it be nice … if the job were exactly what I am looking for?"

"Wouldn't it be nice … if the interviewer and I really liked each other?"

"Wouldn't it be nice … if I felt relaxed and confident during the interview?"

Another example: You are selling your home, and the realtors are bringing prospective buyers over today. You tell yourself:

"Wouldn't it be nice … if these were the dream buyers for our home?"

"Wouldn't it be nice … if we could start searching for a new home?"

The objective in this process is to open up to the positive possibilities in the particular situation you're facing, so that you can manifest them. It is a beginning process that will move you out of resistance and into the realm of the possible.

Alignment Exercise

This exercise is designed to remind you that there are good feelings in what you are currently experiencing, even if you may not acknowledge those good feelings initially.

- Identify how you are feeling on a scale of one to ten, with one being poor and ten being great.

- Wherever the number is on this scale, your intent is to raise your energy vibration as high as you can by the end of the exercise.

- Write down the specific successes you have had in the last week. Successes are anything you did or experienced that gave you a good feeling. For example: You finished a work project and were given accolades for it. Or, your child accomplished a milestone, and you were able to be a part of it. Or, you simply cleaned out a drawer, and the feeling of organization felt wonderful! It's important that you *feel what you are writing about*, so that you are not just recalling particular events.

- Close your eyes, take a deep breath, and bring back the feeling of wellbeing you experienced from this event.

- Experience the good feeling emotion for a minute or two with each success you write down.

- Now, write down *what you currently feel* as you remember each success.

- Since you have just revisited what recently felt good to you, you are likely to feel better and be higher on your emotional scale.

What did you learn about yourself by engaging in *Pivoting, Wouldn't it be nice?,* and the Alignment Exercise? Write down what you are taking away from these experiences. My hope is that you will discover how powerful you are and how much control you have in your life.

ALIGNMENT AND INTERNAL GUIDANCE PARENTING

Once you have practiced listening to and following your own Internal Guidance System and using the exercises regarding more positive thinking, you will have the tools to inspire your children and help them use their IGS. Your power of influence as a parent originates from your alignment, your joy. The practice of returning to alignment when life causes you to move out of alignment enables you to retrieve your power and positive manifesting. When you're in alignment and connected to your Source, you are able to be an inspiration to others, especially your children.

NOTES

CHAPTER 3

Teaching Your Children to Know What's Best for Them

As I was busying myself becoming a new parent, I knew I wanted to be a really good mother. I wanted to teach my kids the right path by drawing from my own life experiences. But the panic set in as I realized that my children might not conform to my vision of what I wanted for them. I wanted them to have integrity; to be organized, creative, independent, thoughtful, and honest; to have clear boundaries; and to appreciate their world. Most of all, I wanted them to know their interior world, which would guide them on their highest path in life. In other words, I wanted them to learn what I was still in the process of learning myself: how to trust their Internal Guidance System so they could follow what was best for them.

But as a new mom, I also worried. What if my kids strayed from my expert advice I still felt I needed to impart and they didn't comply? What would happen to them if they made poor choices on their own? How would I steer them back to the right path? I was enough of a control freak in those days to feel that if they didn't go along with my parental guidance, the consequences could be overwhelming. Yes, I followed my own IGS, but I didn't have the experience in child rearing to know how to relate my knowledge of Internal Guidance to my kids … yet.

So I initially turned to more mainstream sources. I set out on a quest to collect the most noteworthy parenting books. Written by parenting experts who advocated various traditional parenting methods, these books would surely show me the way. I loved looking at all the books that decorated my pretty bookshelf. The interesting thing is that I never opened any of these books once they reached my bookshelf. I meant to, I desperately wanted to, but I literally couldn't do it. When my arm reached up to grab a perfectly safe-looking parenting book, my arm became paralyzed in midair. The stress of cracking open one of those books was too much, and I couldn't figure out why. This frustrating exercise went on for months!

Finally, the day came when I scooped all of the books off the shelf into grocery bags and gave them away. I had been listening to and trusting my own heart for so long that I figured there must be a reason why I couldn't read the books. I was left with one clear option: I was going to have to make every parenting decision, every choice regarding my children, from my heart and from love, showing them how to find their own truths. This way, I would never make a wrong decision, because I don't believe that you can make a wrong choice when you listen to your heart. Perhaps the parenting experts would disapprove, but my decision became clear. Bringing up my kids based on my own Internal Guidance System, and teaching them to use theirs, was the way that felt absolutely right.

As my spiritual studies progressed, I knew there was so much I could teach my children. It wouldn't consist of telling them what decisions they should make, and it wouldn't be predicated on my telling them I had all the answers and all the experience. Instead, I would give them the tools to find and know their own path, their own reasons for being here. I would teach them how to trust themselves completely and know that their lives and all of their experiences happen because of them, not in spite of them.

But first I had to focus on my own intentions. What kind of relationship did I want to have with my children?

SETTING YOUR INTENTION

When my kids were very young, I decided to define and *intend* the kind of relationship I wanted with them; I was slightly terrified to leave it to chance. I knew I wanted to be emotionally close, spend as much time with each child as possible, and teach the kids to follow their own paths by listening to their own Internal Guidance Systems. I also very much wanted a friendship with them once they were grown, envisioning myself being very involved in their lives. To achieve this, my parenting would have to be conscious and deliberate, with a clear outcome in mind.

By observing friends who had older children, I was able to clearly define the kind of relationship I wanted with my own kids. Those relationships served as a model. I saw the fun these families were having together, the easy communication they shared, and a general dynamic between them that felt good to me. I knew that in order to have what these friends had with their kids, I didn't need to parent like they parented or know anything about their daily lives. I only had to be clear in the outcome I wanted and hold my intent.

My studies of the Law of Attraction and the Universe have shown me that having an intention propels the energy forward, toward creating what you want. To be clear, we are always moving forward, but intent is the powerful energy that serves as our "rocket engine." I clearly intended what I wanted and also how I was going to get there. Life is a process, and I was going to have to hold this intention in my consciousness as I moved forward and lived daily life with my family.

How was I going to get there? I wondered. I knew the end result I wanted, but this end result would be the sum of all the interactions with my children during their childhood. I had to handle every situation holding that "end result" vision. My intent wasn't something I thought about every day. Once I had clearly set it into motion, it was held in my consciousness. It was always there and came into my conscious mind when particular situations came up with the kids. At those times, I was reminded of my intent and could then determine whether or not I was moving in the direction I wanted, based upon how I was feeling.

Parenting from my highest self, which I knew would get me to my goal, could only be determined by me. This would mean following my Internal Guidance System and being aware of how I was feeling as I was raising my children and dealing with whatever came up.

Just about every situation in a parent's daily life offers a choice: to be fully present to your child and offer a deliberate response, or to respond reactively. As I was learning to be more aware and deliberate, I had many *reactive responses*. What is a reactive response? Those knee-jerk reactions in which words and body language are regretted once they have been acted out or spoken. These responses left me feeling like I hadn't been helpful to my child, hadn't made them feel my love and support. And such responses had also not imparted any wisdom or teaching. My post-reaction feelings weren't good, and this was my indicator that I was not following through with my intent of fostering a close relationship. I was also not getting what I wanted, which was cooperation from the kids and a desired behavior from them. Lesson learned: Children react to how you react to them.

I soon discovered that when a situation arose and I was deliberately present for my child, when I took the time to really listen and support them and chose what I said and how I offered support, I felt good about my parenting. I was confident that I was moving in the direction of my goals and intent. In those instances I learned that clarity attracts clarity. And when I approached a situation being clear about the level of cooperation that I wanted from my kids, that is what I usually got back from them.

To sum it up: I began with a clear and loving intent toward my children, and they always felt whatever energy I sent their way. I held a vision of cooperation and an intention for whatever resolution was needed. I deliberately chose my responses and was conscious of staying on track to maintain a pattern of good communication and issue resolution that would support my intent in that moment and in the future.

What kind of relationship do you want with your children? Do you want to be emotionally close with them? Do you want your kids to feel comfortable making their own choices while learning from your example? Is there another parent/child relationship that you admire and would like to emulate?

Why not take some time to write down what your intentions are as a parent: How do you want to relate to your children? What do you want your kids to learn from your interactions with them? Next, we'll consider the tools you can offer your child so that he or she will be better prepared to follow their own Internal Guidance System.

THE TOOLS: FEELINGS, TRUST, AND INTENTION

After we become comfortable using our own IGS, we can teach our children how to use theirs. Where do we begin? With feelings—specifically, teaching children to pay attention to what their feelings are communicating to them.

Young children are keenly aware of how they feel. They will rarely hesitate to tell others when they are happy, unhappy, or want a specific need met. They come into this life without filters, believing that whatever they desire should be granted them. They unconsciously know that they have an Internal Guidance System, and they use it in all of the choices they make. In animals, we call this sense of knowing *instinct*. Children "follow the fun," so to speak, and they intrinsically know that in their happiness all is well and things work out for them. Your child will know that whatever feels good to them is the right course of action, and they will continue knowing this until they are told otherwise.

Children also have a radar or instinct to help keep them safe. They know when something or someone feels bad to them, and they will want to keep their distance. A child's radar sometimes becomes very apparent when a stranger is present. Often, a child may have a lot of resistance to this stranger but will not be able to tell you why. It will be their IGS working. **As a parent, we don't have to create our children's IGS. We must help them recognize and use it wisely.**

Each of us is born with an IGS, and we use it from birth. Children trust that what they want is right for them. We can guide them in trusting that when something feels good to them, it is indeed right for them. The temptation for most parents is to want to control and decide for our children, from being fearful because we don't trust that they have an Internal Guidance System—or that they will use it wisely. Teaching your kids to recognize what their IGS is communicating to them is of far greater value than simply telling them what choice they ought to make.

You can teach your children how to set their intentions by asking them what they want. If you take them through the process of verbalizing what they want in the moment, and also what they want at a future time, you can teach them to discern the difference. You can help them to develop the ability to look farther down the road to where they want to be and what they ultimately want to have, and learn to create goals for themselves.

How does an intention differ from a goal? My studies and experience have shown me that *intention is the energy that moves us forward in obtaining our desired goal.* For example, a child may have a certain goal, something they want to accomplish. Perhaps they want to become captain of their soccer team. It will help them to verbalize their intent: "I want and intend to be captain of my team." They can then verbalize what it will take to accomplish their goal: "I will become the best player on my team." Then, it is important that they are *in alignment* with their desire and intent in order for it to manifest. Being in alignment means that they believe that they deserve and can accomplish their goal, and there are no negative emotions, such a fear, thwarting their intention.

If we can teach our children to know what their feelings are indicating to them, to trust the validity of those feelings, and to focus on their intentions, we can help them transition into puberty, the teenage years, and adulthood knowing that they possess everything inside of themselves to create their ideal lives. They will never feel that they need to rely on others or any external forces to create what they want.

DO CHILDREN REALLY KNOW BEST?

We do a great disservice to our children by teaching them that the answers to their problems and uncertainties exist within other people and other things. This is an illusion and goes against the natural laws of our Universe. When we convince our children that we know better and that we have the life experience to chart their course, we feed this illusion. The truth is that each person's answers, no matter what their age, are found within themselves. Still, most parents tend to have their own ideas about what they feel is reasonable for their children and what they want them to be exposed to.

I am not suggesting that as parents we shouldn't guide our children; what I'm suggesting is that we teach them to be aware of and use their Internal Guidance System. Keeping kids safe is one thing. Allowing them to discover their own path—often by trial and error, but increasingly by trusting their IGS—is quite another.

Teaching your kids to make their own choices, even if you don't agree with those choices, helps them fine-tune their IGS. For example: your son wants a hand-held videogame that you feel is too violent and a waste of his time. How to handle the situation? Encourage him to be aware of his feelings while playing the game. Then, ask him a few questions: How does the violence make him feel? What is it about the game that inspires him and makes him feel good? Why does he want to play this particular game? How will playing this game help him learn something? Thinking about these questions will help your child tap into his IGS and become more aware of his feelings and motivations.

Certainly as parents we are required to set certain parameters for our kids, especially when it comes to their safety. With that said, it is always important to take your child's feelings into consideration and to allow him to make decisions for himself, while also teaching him to be aware of the consequences of those decisions. Such awareness is an important part of listening to his IGS.

What does it mean to teach your child to listen to and follow her IGS? It means teaching her to trust their first impulse toward an action that makes her feel "this is the right thing for me to do." When your child is *in alignment* and feeling good, her impulses come from the Universe (Higher Self) and thus are for her highest good. Any impulse that is felt when *not* in alignment is not a message from the Universe, but from the reactive state. And any action based on such an impulse will *not* result in getting what she wants. It won't be her best choice.

Children will instinctively choose actions and behaviors that serve their highest good, but they will also react to their environment, which will *not* serve their highest good. For example: your daughter doesn't want to participate in a group activity at school, but prefers to create what she pleases on the sidelines. Her teacher's first reaction is to insist that all the kids do the outlined activity, and you agree. One course of action would be to force your daughter to participate against her wishes. The other is to allow her to be independent because that is what is pleasing her at the moment; she is following her IGS toward her highest good.

Let's look at another example: A child has the impulse to hit her brother. It is safe to say that most children will not hit another person when they are *in alignment*. Such an action generally comes out of anger, which only happens when someone is *out of alignment*. Any action taken from non-alignment will not serve a child and will not get them what they want.

When your child acts out of anger, it is an ideal time for you to teach them the difference between acting from alignment and being connected to their highest self—that is, feeling good—and choosing behaviors that come from feeling bad. In my generation, we were taught, "Think before you act." I believe it is actually more appropriate to teach our kids, "Feel before you act."

So a conversation between you and your six-year-old who hit her little brother might go something like this:

You: *Do you know why you hit your brother?*

Your daughter: *He grabbed my crayons and made me mad!*

You: *How did your brother react when you hit him?*

Daughter: *Well, he hit me back.*

You: *Did any of this get your crayons back?*

Daughter: *Nope.*

You: *Next time your brother does something you don't like, try and think about what you want. In this case, it was your crayons. You already know that getting mad only makes your brother mad and doesn't get your crayons back. So, think about your heart and what would make your heart feel better. All of your answers are in your heart. When you and I draw pictures of hearts with your crayons, what does the heart picture mean?*

Daughter: *Love.*

You: *Yes, it means love. I would like you to think about how love can get what you want from your brother. Maybe that means you ask him nicely. Or you find other crayons. Remember that the quickest way to get what you want will always be by not getting mad. Try distracting your brother and making him laugh.*

ENVISION YOUR CHILD AS HER HIGHEST SELF

Holding the highest vision for your child—envisioning and believing in her ability to make good decisions and create a healthy, happy, productive life—will help ensure that she will do so. When your energy is loving and supportive, you can *hold this space* for your child on an energetic level. This means that with your encouragement and positive energy, you can help facilitate the life she wants. Regardless of her current situation, you can always hold the highest vision for your child.

For example: Your daughter may be struggling in school, not achieving what she is capable of. You want her to do better, but when you continue to focus on the fact that she is failing to meet your expectations, she is unlikely to move forward. Instead, it's essential that you focus on her, as you want her to be. This means envisioning her as a better, happier student—and treating her as such. She will react and be inspired by whatever thoughts and feelings you're sending her way, be it positive or negative.

Since our ability to be a positive influence for our children is only possible when we are in alignment, we must find a way to maintain our alignment no matter what situation our child is in. Again, we can only inspire others, including our children, when we are in alignment. When we feel good, our children are inspired to reach for that feeling, as well.

As we discussed in chapter two, the Law of Attraction enables us to envision others as their highest selves and to facilitate positive change in our relationships by giving us whatever we are thinking about. With our own children, such a process of envisioning is particularly powerful. When you envision your child achieving what he or she is capable of and becoming his or her highest self, you send your support and loving energy to facilitate that actually happening. As you continue to engage in this process of envisioning, your supportive attitude toward your child becomes the dominant energy between the two of you. And that allows your child to make choices that will ultimately be life-affirming and beneficial.

ALLOWING YOUR CHILD TO MAKE CHOICES

We are all here to express our freedom, and children intrinsically know this. Each of us is here to live our highest joy and to have the freedom to create our own paths. But how do we, as parents, balance freedom with safety? How do we allow our children to make choices on their own so that they grow up knowing who they are as they reach for their highest selves—and at the same time discourage them from engaging in what we believe to be dangerous or risky behavior?

There will be times when your kids make choices that don't appear to you to be their highest (best) choice. Such choices, although they may seem to be unwise or bad, are an important part of a child's evolution. None of us can know exactly what we want until we experience life fully, and this includes experiencing what we *don't* want. Children need this experience. Your children will inevitably do things that they'll discover aren't as much fun as they thought, or they may be faced with unpleasant consequences from an action they took. Part of any child's learning includes sifting through the choices and desires in their lives to create what they want.

If we can teach our children to use their Internal Guidance Systems and encourage them to make choices without judging them, we will contribute to their growth. In order to do this, we must first remove the "good" and "bad" labels, which are judgments. Rather than pronouncing a certain behavior "good" or "bad," we can pose this question to our children: "Does this decision (or action) serve you or not, meaning does it take you in a direction you want to go?"

What do I mean by an action or decision "serving you"? *If you feel good about your decision, and you made your choice when you were in alignment, then it serves you* in some way; if it does not feel good and the choice was made when you were not in alignment, then it doesn't serve you.

For example: Your son wants to quit taking piano lessons, which previously brought him joy. He still loves music but has discovered that playing the guitar and writing his own songs is more creative and more fun. His new choice will serve his creativity and expansion because this new choice sprung from his alignment and joy regarding his new creative outlet.

But what about the choices that *do not serve* your child? For example: Your son chooses to periodically skip school. The natural consequence of his actions is that he has to repeat the classes in order to make up lost credits. He may be able to take the missed classes in summer school, but he may not be able to do so in time to graduate with his class. So how do you respond as his parent? Once he has made a choice that certainly appears to have not been a good one, it serves no one to suffer over it. What's done is done, and it is time to move on. In other words, I am not a believer in adding to the natural consequences when a child makes a less-than-ideal choice.

I don't believe that it serves a child to be punished further by losing all of his privileges. If a child is left with nothing, he will become so out of alignment that he won't be able to create anything productive. Does this mean that you should never impose consequences when your child engages in negative behavior? Not necessarily. I imposed consequences when I felt disrespected by my child or felt that their act was clearly reckless. However, I did not punish when I encountered a situation where my son or daughter acted when they were in alignment and made a decision *they* felt good about, but which I didn't happen to agree with. Each parent has to look at these situations individually and decide in the moment what they want to teach their child.

We can help our children move forward by encouraging them to become clear on *what they want* based on having experienced *what they don't want*. Life is always about looking ahead, not back. Allowing your children to experience their own consequences isn't easy, but it is liberating because it frees you from the need to fix things for them. On the other hand, attempting to save your children from life's trials and tribulations only holds them back from discovering who they are and what they want from life. Our first impulse as parents is to protect and defend our kids, but with practice we can instead stand beside them and allow them to grow by letting them listen to their Internal Guidance Systems and make their own choices.

When we trust our IGS as well as our child's, we no longer measure their success according to how well they comply with our demands. Rather, we take joy in their freedom.

BEING THE EXAMPLE

I did not learn how to parent in one fell swoop. I learned how to parent with each individual child and each individual situation that came up in our lives. Every challenge, no matter how trying at the time, offered us opportunities to learn together.

As the children were growing up, I did what most parents do. I thought of the qualities I wanted them to learn and embody. My teachings and guidance were always about being aware of what my kids would take with them out into the world. So I was mindful of exemplifying, in my own behavior and energy vibration, those qualities I wanted them to develop. Being an example to your children is the most important teaching tool because children watch more than they listen.

And even more powerfully, kids respond to our energy vibration by what they feel from us. What I sent their way in my thoughts, beliefs, and expectations had the most profound effect on my children. Again, we inspire from being in alignment or *high vibration*. Over time and with experience, I was able to show my kids through my vibration and behavior how I dealt with life's situations. I did this by demonstrating calmness and non-judgment when challenging situations arose. And I backed this up with some advice about judging others and being judged.

When my children were tempted to judge others or were judged by others, I did my best to make them aware of the bigger picture. When they were judged, I encouraged them to realize that other people project and lash out because of what is happening in their own personal experience. And when my kids were tempted to judge others, I reminded them that they cannot know the life path of another person. I encouraged them to check in with their Internal Guidance Systems and find a way to offer compassion, rather than reacting with vengeance or anger.

I felt it was very important to show my kids that life's challenges could be dealt with in a mostly non-reactive manner. We always have a choice in how we act or react, and our choices powerfully influence our children. For example: When my treasured sports car was rear-ended, it sustained damage, but the other person's car was nearly totaled. I didn't get angry, and I felt I was very lucky to have not been injured. I felt appreciation that I was able to return home and be nurtured. I wrote a letter of compassion to the other driver, and my kids took note of how I handled that situation.

Of course, there have been times when my behavior wasn't a hundred percent exemplary. Life is a practice, and practice is what we continually do to become who we want to be. Your children will always call you out when they see a contradiction between what you say and what you do. They will always keep you accountable. Mine did. There were times when I set guidelines for one of the kids, and when the time came to follow through I had forgotten the details so I didn't require them to comply. One of the other kids felt it was unfair for me not to impose the same guidelines for their sibling as they had experienced. I agreed; fair is fair.

The bottom line: I discovered that being the kind of person I want to inspire my kids to be, and living the life I want to inspire them to live, was the best rule of thumb. This doesn't mean being on your guard all the time; it means being a relaxed parent who makes deliberate and conscious decisions toward your kids.

THE FUNDAMENTALS OF IGS PARENTING

As you begin to consider the spiritual and practical advantages of using your Internal Guidance System to guide your parenting decisions—and allowing your child to use her IGS to make choices—let's take a moment to review the fundamentals. The following are the essential principles on which IGS parenting is based.

- *Set your intention for the type of relationship you want with your child.* You can set your intention for what you want each day, as your children grow and develop. And you can also set your intention for the long run, when your kids are grown. Intend the qualities you want them to embody. Intend the level of communication you desire with them, the emotional closeness. Review all that is important to you in your parenting and relationship with your kids, and specifically intend all of it. It can be helpful to write down your intentions to have as a reference.

- *Teach your child to listen to and trust his feelings.* Remind him to be aware of what he is feeling. How does each choice feel when he considers it? Is he propelled forward toward a certain choice because it feels good, or does he want to move away from that choice because it doesn't feel good?

- *Teach your child to consider her intentions.* What kind of person does she want to be? What kinds of friendships does she hope to enjoy? What does she want to learn? Make her aware that her intentions carry the energy—the power—that moves her forward toward what she wants.

- *Envision your child embodying her highest self.* Holding the highest vision of what you want for your child, regardless of his current situation, will inspire him to rise to a higher potential.

- *Give your child the freedom to make choices.* Words don't teach; life experience does. Allow your child to discover what she wants by experiencing some of what she doesn't want. This is how she clarifies her desires. What may appear as a mistake will serve as a clarification.

- *Be the example of the values and behavior you want your child to inherit.* Your energy vibration is your most powerful influence. Understand that being in alignment is where your power as a parent lies. Always show your child the behavior you want him to emulate as you encounter life's challenges.

These are the basics. In the following chapters, we'll explore specific issues that arise throughout a child's life— and how you can employ IGS parenting to ensure a happier, more rewarding life for your children.

NOTES

Giving Kids the Power to Succeed in School

In this chapter, we're going to explore the challenge of allowing kids to set their own educational goals, the difficulty of letting go of your parental expectations, and how IGS helps both parents and kids do their part in this interconnected process.

As we discussed in chapter two, your vibration is more powerful than any action you can take. You will inspire others—including your children—by being in your highest place of joy, calm, and inner stillness as you envision and intend the best for your child. But how does this actually work in the real world? What if you have cause to worry about your child's grades and school activities? Will trusting the Universe, visualizing your child's highest self, sending him your most positive vibration, and teaching him to trust his IGS be enough to make a difference? As parents, we can't help but want our kids to do well in school because we believe that their success as students, their ability to develop good study habits and interact respectfully with teachers and peers, will serve them well in whatever career they choose. So can we be calm and joyful as we watch them avoiding their homework or not giving their studies enough attention?

When my son, Dustin, was in middle school, I found myself ignoring the IGS principles I had developed over the previous years because I suddenly found myself fearful. I was frustrated by his behavior and lack of focus in school, and I allowed myself to be reactive. I was pushing him harder as his grades got worse, and his efforts slackened. As I watched myself going down the emotional path of a reactive parent, getting nowhere with my son, I remembered that I had a choice.

I asked myself: What did I want for Dustin? I wanted him to be a better student, have a kinder voice, and be a calmer person. After years of trying to push, demand, and punish him into a more successful life, I had to find a better way. Clearly, what I was doing was just not working. I was constantly scrutinizing his grades and insisting on certain behaviors, and he was only pushing back. Our relationship was in serious jeopardy. I slowly started to focus on who Dustin really was: a unique soul, a person on his own path, an individual who was not here to please me but to find his own way in the world. Reminding myself of this essential truth was a tough one. But then I started to visualize Dustin succeeding at school, being happy, and making his own choices. I saw him using the Internal Guidance System I had taught him about, yet hadn't let him use because of my own fears regarding his success.

One fine day, the Universe gave me the opportunity to not only visualize Dustin's success but to trust him with his own life and wellbeing.

GIVING DUSTIN'S POWER BACK TO HIM

Sometimes as a parent you have the realization that you are done. Not with parenting, nor with your child, but with fighting a battle that can't be won. It took me a while to acknowledge this fact as I found myself headstrong in a battle with Dustin and out of touch with what I was trying to teach him. I was convinced that I was being a good and supportive parent, even though our relationship continued to deteriorate. It seemed that much of what I had learned about the Law of Attraction and Universal truths had not been fully integrated into my parenting. I had given my children a solid base upon which to build, but I needed to go deeper. And I needed to really practice what I preached with my son, who was now fourteen.

Dustin always seemed to be an old, wise soul. His mellow demeanor and generally easygoing ways had made me sense his wisdom and maturity, although I was often frustrated with his noncompliance. Dustin's early childhood was, for the most part, very happy, with a few bumps successfully ironed out over time. In middle school, however, he seemed to continually find himself in some sort of trouble. I often felt that the school was overreacting because the trouble never involved malicious behavior toward another child. The exception was when Dustin physically prevented the school bully from punching a handicapped child. The principal was forced to discipline Dustin but made it discreetly clear that all was well. Dustin often seemed to be in the right place to help a kid in imminent danger. These school experiences helped show me that my son had his heart in the right place, regardless of his academic performance.

Fast-forward to Dustin at age fifteen. At that point, I had taught him well about following his own IGS, but I wasn't allowing him to use it where school was concerned. I had allowed myself to think I needed to control the situation. I don't know why I thought there were exceptions. For example, whenever he struggled in a class, I was immediately in contact with his counselor to find a solution. In one case, he was mandated to attend a tutorial class before and after school. In another, I enrolled him in an extra math class, which did not go well. Although Dustin was more or less willing to go along with my decisions, there was no sign of him committing to his own success.

In my well-meaning effort to keep Dustin accountable and on top of his workload, I required that we regularly check grades and assignments together online. This was my bright idea, and it always resulted in a fight. If I saw a missed assignment, I wanted to know why, which always led to Dustin becoming defensive. Often, so much time had passed that he simply couldn't recall the incident and would say something like, "But Mom, it's been two months!" It took far too long for me to realize that this so-called accountability exercise was not improving Dustin's grades and instead was hurting our relationship. Eventually, I couldn't even mention school because I knew my remarks would lead to a confrontation.

I realized that I was trying to rescue a child who didn't need rescuing. Dustin simply was in the process of finding his own way, and I was trying to control both his actions and the outcome.

It was at this precise moment in time that I was intensively restudying the Universal Law of Attraction for my life coaching certification. Everything I had learned about following one's own Internal Guidance System was being received by me in a new and expanded way. I was taking classes and studying from books and listening to audio CDs. Then, one day I popped the latest disc into my car player, remembering the feelings of frustration over what to do with my son. All of the answers that I had asked for in order to help Dustin were there, miraculously waiting for me. On the CD, a mother asked how she could help her son do better in school, manage his life in a more organized way, and so on. The answer, in short, was that any child fares better when they are allowed the leeway to use their IGS to maneuver their way. I was reminded that intrinsically every child knows his path on some level, even though allowing kids to follow their own path doesn't necessarily meet parental or societal standards.

What I knew, practiced, and taught others was what I now needed to apply, learn, and do myself in relation to Dustin.

It was time for me to give Dustin his life and his power back. That evening, I sat nervously at dinner, wondering if I would be able to express to Dustin the important teachings that the CD had reminded me of. I wasn't sure I could pull it off. I began by making a general comment about IGS. Dustin wasn't sure what I was getting at and asked me what I was talking about. There was no turning back. I took a deep breath, said a quick prayer to my angels to please speak through me, and with as much calm as I could muster, I lovingly said to Dustin: "I trust you to know what is right for you. You have your own Internal Guidance System that will never fail you. You already know how to listen to it, and I am going to let you. You will hear your highest path when you feel good and are happy. Everything that you need is inside of you. Listen to your messages and impulses. Feel which direction you are inspired to move toward. It is all there. What may look to me like a failure is simply a judgment on my part, and I will do my best not to judge your choices. I am giving you back control of your school life on a silver platter. I will no longer be checking online to see your grades or assignments. Ever. It is not my business; you are in the process of deciding whom you want to be. I am not deserting you. I am here to support you, as I always have. All you need to do is ask."

Dustin just looked at me with shock and disbelief. Finally, he smiled, and I could see he was trying to process what had just happened. He got up from the dinner table and came over to give me a huge bear hug. My fifteen-year-old was already six-foot-three, and trust me, when he hugs it *is* a bear hug. "Thank you so much, Mom," he said. "I will never forget this."

He smiled again, and I could tell a huge weight had been lifted off his shoulders and our relationship. Off he went up the stairs while I sat at the dinner table in shock.

As I mentioned earlier, my Law of Attraction studies have taught me that how you see others has a profound influence on your experience of them. I had been sending out to the Universe, and to Dustin as well, my thoughts and feelings of a struggling student who couldn't get his life in order. Since the Universe will always, without exception, give back to you what you think and therefore feel, I was only able to experience the negative aspects of Dustin's school performance until I changed how I viewed him.

Let me expand on this: Each of us experiences others in our own unique way, which is based solely on what we expect and believe of them or about them. **In order for me to have a different experience of Dustin, I needed to start seeing him in a different way—in the way I wanted to see him, not in the context of what was currently happening.** This takes vision and practice.

Have you ever described to someone your experience of a mutual friend or acquaintance and had them tell you that they don't see this person in that way at all? The discrepancy between your feelings and the other person's feelings about the same individual is due to different sets of beliefs and expectations, which result in your perspective. The Law of Attraction is absolute and makes no exceptions. You will experience others (and also the world) based on what you are feeling—meaning, what you think and believe.

Once I gave his power back to him, I consciously and completely changed my vision of Dustin. I practiced thoughts of seeing him where I wanted him to be, not where he currently was. I projected a vision of his success—a vision of him doing well in school, being resourceful and happy. I knew I could inspire him energetically and that I would be happier holding this positive vision of Dustin. I also knew he would be happier because he would be feeling my highest vision of him. This would be the most powerful gift I could give him.

Dustin is now a senior in high school. I never again checked his grades and never wanted to; I knew that it might cause me to become judgmental. I truly had given him back his power, with no strings attached and no expectations from me about how all of it would turn out. Being attached to a certain outcome is limiting in that it prevents the Universe from doing its highest work, which may very well be a better outcome than you can envision. I finally trusted Dustin, and I trusted life's process.

Ever since that evening at the dinner table, Dustin and I have never had a fight about school. In fact, he now feels safe discussing his schoolwork with me. The change in his attitude toward school was not immediate. He went through his process of defining whom he wanted to be, but his grades improved dramatically over time, and he now says he feels empowered and in control of his own life and what happens within it.

Dustin is following his own Internal Guidance System and feels good about it. If a grade in a particular class starts to slip, he handles it. He never felt good about having his grades go down, but now he knows that he controls the outcome and Mom won't be stepping into the middle of it. This has given him a feeling of empowerment and being in control of his experiences. I trust Dustin to handle his own life, and I trust that his life will be the outcome of what he believes it will be. I needed to back off and let him decide it all for himself, and I am so glad I did.

Giving Dustin back his life didn't mean that I gave up the influence and inspiration I had to offer—quite the contrary. Instead, I was now going to offer it from my true place of power, which is from my joy and alignment. And I would also be holding the highest vision of my son. I wouldn't trade this feeling of peace for anything in the world.

DUSTIN'S SIDE OF THE STORY

In case you think that I may be painting too rosy a picture of how Dustin came to take back his power and use his Internal Guidance System to guide his life, here is his version of how he made that transition and what it meant to him. I asked him to share in his own words.

A few years ago, a very peculiar thing happened to me. Everything was going according to a normal day in the life of a middle school student. But when the time came to sit down with the family to eat dinner, I noticed my mom was kind of looking at me strangely. I thought nothing of it and continued to serve myself a big ole helping of mac 'n' cheese, and as I took that first bite, I heard the words, "Dustin, I am giving you your life back." I was utterly confused, but my mom's seriousness kept my attention.

She went on to explain that she was no longer going to check my grades or bug me about such things as cleaning my room or hanging up my towels—you know, the little things. After her explanation, I was left confused, but I was also happy to know that she wasn't going to bug me about my homework anymore, so I certainly wasn't going to ask any questions.

My mother and I have been through our ups and downs just like every other mother and son, but God knows I didn't make it easy for her. As a preteen, I never seemed to do very well in school, and to make matters worse, I always seemed to find trouble. (Mom says it was minor.) I couldn't help it. It wasn't like I was a bad kid, because the trouble I was getting into was never ill-intentioned. One could say I was just having a good time doing some things we weren't allowed to do. School also never seemed very important to me; it was just something I had to do and basically one more thing Mom bugged me about.

Before my mother "gave me my life back," our relationship was strained at times. She would continuously bother me about school and my grades, neither of which was going very well. As a result, our conversations didn't go well either. The fights with my mom seemed ongoing and never-ending, so arguing was something I simply anticipated. Bottom line: it wasn't motivating me to do better in school, because the only one who seemed to care was Mom.

I can only imagine how fed up my mother was with my crap. She had tried everything to get me back on track, and little did she know that the most effective thing she could do was nothing. She simply had to let go and allow me to rule my own life. This was big news for me, not only because there was to be much less fighting between us, but also because she was going to stop watching over my shoulder all the time. This is when I really learned about and integrated her teachings about my Internal Guidance System, and I also realized my success and happiness—now and later in life—was entirely up to me and not my mother. I also learned that when left to my own judgment, I can make the right decision. I know when I'm doing the right thing for myself because I feel good, internally, about the choice I've made. That is my IGS guiding me to my truth.

Having my life meant that, literally, life was completely in my hands now. How well I did in school, my relationships with others—everything was all within me. Although it felt a little weird at first to actually care about some important things I had been ignoring for a while, I quickly started seeing results. I noticed that my grades were going up, and the motivation that had been lacking for so long was now apparent. When my mom "let go," I uncovered a newfound *self-confidence, and it became obvious that the only thing that held me back previously was myself. I realized that I had to use and experience my Internal Guidance System in order to trust myself.*

These days, I try to do what I feel is best in order to better myself. Some people spend their whole lives looking for someone else to tell them what to do or what is right, but the truth is that the answer lies in your own heart. No matter how grueling the task may be, when you use your Internal Guidance System you will be able to conquer anything.

A CHECKING-UP CHECKLIST

I have come to realize that we parents have access to way too much information about our children, and this information doesn't always serve us. When I was a student, my parents couldn't check my grades online. There was no online. These days, however, we can readily check our kids' grades, assignments, and missed assignments. Thanks to the Internet, most of us have ongoing access to up-to-the-minute reports about our kids' educational progress. Given our current technology, it's a wonder that our children's classrooms aren't equipped with closed-circuit cameras so that we can check up on them whenever the parental urge arises.

But as my experience with Dustin reveals, constantly checking up on our kids doesn't produce the results we want; it can make us want to control the uncontrollable. Giving them the freedom to make their own choices does. Dustin and I will never forget the day I gave him back his power—the day I decided to trust him, knowing that he could count on his own Internal Guidance System and follow his own life path. It took years for me to get to that point, though. Initially, if Dustin's actions didn't match what I thought was best for him, I tried to get him to do it my way, which never worked. So I stopped checking up on him, and instead he began to check up on himself. If he forgot to turn in an assignment or study for a test, he had to experience the consequences and take responsibility. He learned from his own experience how his actions produce specific results. He also learned to focus on what he wanted to achieve and to figure out what works best for him in terms of how he can achieve it. He did all that figuring out without my checking up on him!

As you learn to trust your Internal Guidance System, and as your child learns to trust his, you might want to consult this checklist to help you consider where you stand when it comes to the "checking-up-on-your-child's-schoolwork challenge":

- When your child returns from his school day, do you routinely question him about what and how much homework he has? YES____ NO____

- When you notice that your child is not studying or doing homework in the evening, do you question her about why she's not working on her schoolwork? YES____ NO____

- If your child receives less than A's or B's on his report card, do you automatically make an appointment with his teacher to see what the problem is? YES____ NO____

- Do you constantly remind your child that if she doesn't receive enough A's on her report cards, she won't get into the best colleges? YES____ NO____

- When friends discuss their child's grades or school performance, do you mentally compare it with your child's? YES____ NO____

If you checked "yes" to any of these questions, you probably need to check in with your IGS and focus on allowing your child to be guided by his own. Parenting seems easy when our children happily comply with what we ask and expect. But there comes a time in every child's life when they will no longer do what their parents want them to do or act in the manner their parents expect. This is the time when, if you haven't done so already, you need to teach your child about following their IGS and striving for his highest good. Rest assured that they will always find their way when their Internal Guidance System guides them, and you can facilitate this ongoing practice by allowing them more freedom in the process.

OFFERING INFLUENCE AND INSPIRATION FROM YOUR PLACE OF POWER

As I mentioned previously, you are the greatest inspiration to your child when you have a high vibration, meaning that you are feeling happy and in alignment. Your place of power is found in your alignment, and you must find a way to maintain it even when your child is displaying a behavior that threatens to get you *out of* alignment. This can easily happen when it comes to issues related to school.

We want our kids to feel supported, so how do we offer our support with the greatest chance of it being received well? This process is generally easiest when your child is young, before they enter puberty and your questions appear invasive. Young kids usually welcome the attention when you ask them about their homework or what they did in school that day. They often take pride in their accomplishments and want to share with you what they've learned. This is the time to integrate the level of care you have for them. Pay close, caring attention to what they tell you about school. Ask them about their day, what their teacher talked about or demonstrated, what they didn't understand or had problems with, and whether what they did that day was fun or interesting. Focus on *listening* to what they have to tell you. Your children will learn from experience that you care and are there to support them.

This will greatly serve you later on when your questions about how things are going at school are met with resistance. Preteens and teens will likely know and appreciate that you care about them and how they're doing in school, even though it may appear to you that they're annoyed by your interest. This is not the time to stop asking how things are going and showing that you care, but it is the time to resist pushing through any resistance that your child displays. Your pushing will only create more resistance.

Remember: You won't be able to maintain your alignment when you are pushing against anything unwanted. When you are out of alignment, you cannot influence and inspire your child or anyone else.

I never stopped asking my teen or preteen about their school day, their friends, or their activities because I still wanted them to know I was interested in their lives. Often my questions were greeted with a less than vague answer: "What did you do today?" "Nothing." Only when they were in the best of moods, or wanted something, would they be willing to tell me what went on in their classes that day. As I mentioned in the Dustin story, I eventually learned to back off and allow them the freedom to manage their time, workload, and activities.

Your child needs to know that you trust them. If you *don't* trust them to manage their time and their homework, you must learn to. I learned to trust my kids because trying to control them absolutely did not work. I only got the results I wanted when I allowed them the freedom to learn to manage their own time and choose what to do for themselves and when.

Here are some core guidelines on how to offer inspiration from being in your power—especially with regard to your child's schoolwork:

- Know that in order to influence your child in a positive, healthy way, you must be in alignment.

- Show an authentic interest in your child's schoolwork, without making judgments or setting forth expectations.

- Focus on listening to your child's experiences, feelings, and thoughts about school.

- Be a good role model by demonstrating good time management skills, but don't expect your child to do things your way.

EACH CHILD EVOLVES ACCORDING TO THEIR OWN TIMELINE

When my kids were quite young, I remember having a moment of panic regarding their futures. I thought, "How will I handle it if they don't follow my lead and do what I believe is best for them?" Boy, did I have to give that one up. The fact of the matter is we don't know what is best for our kids; only they do. Often they don't discover what is best for them until the time is right because each child has his or her own intrinsic timeline. But are we aware of that fact—or do we tend to want our kids to do things the way we did them, and to reach certain milestones when it's considered "normal" to do so?

I think that too often we fall prey to believing that our kids must conform to particular life schedules prescribed by our society— especially when it comes to their intellectual and educational development. This parental concern often starts very early on. Moms and dads worry if their babies aren't sitting up, crawling, walking, and talking at the age when their friends' babies accomplish these important milestones. When a child reaches preschool, parents may fret that their son lags behind the others in learning his letters. Or perhaps he is shyer than the other kids and has a harder time adjusting to being in a group. Maybe a kindergartener doesn't keep pace with her classmates as they learn to count. Again, every child develops according to his or her unique timeline. As parents, it serves our children best when we allow for this uniqueness and refrain from pushing our agenda onto our kids.

Once a child starts school, there are guidelines in place, a curriculum that stipulates what a student is expected to learn. Since reading, writing, and math are taught in certain grades and the school and parents have particular expectations, it can be difficult for the child who doesn't conform to the prescribed timeline. Ideally, it would make more sense to allow children to use their own IGS, which permits them to know when they are ready to learn a given subject. But since most traditional school systems aren't set up that way, children must keep up with the others or suffer the consequences—namely, poor grades and disapproval on the part of their peers and parents.

Neither teachers nor parents have control over when kids are ready to learn. Children progress academically when they want to learn and are ready to do so. Certainly we can contribute to a child's progress by offering our encouragement and support, but a child has to enter the educational arena from their own joy and readiness. We can't push against their lack of readiness. No child will "receive an education" if he is not ready for it or doesn't want to receive it, no matter what their age is.

If you have a child who is struggling in school, realize that you don't have control over the pace at which he learns, or whether he ultimately will be successful. Your own IGS will guide you to offer the appropriate support and help your child may need, such as encouragement or tutoring. But it's not within your power to make your child accept this help. He must be ready to accept it. A child in resistance will push against whatever is being offered, so offer what you feel would benefit you child without forcing it and then allow him to progress at his own pace. When he makes the decision to learn, he will.

As we all know, the teenage years can present a specific set of challenges. During this period, we want our kids to start doing well in school because their grades count for college entrance. At a time when their brains are not fully formed or engaged, we expect our kids to perform at their highest level. We tell them that their high school years are critical to their future success and that, for their own good, we expect them to measure up.

Unfortunately, in our culture, teenagers get zero credibility or support for using their own IGS. In fact, I believe many parents would refute the fact that their teen even *has* one. Yet, at this age, it is crucial that they use it, fine-tune it, and trust it.

Encouraging your teen to follow his or her own IGS can be especially trying for parents because we can't help but notice when our kids make choices that we believe are bad ones. Interestingly, though, we also notice that we have absolutely no control over some of these choices. So when your teen puts off writing that essay or spends the evening before an exam goofing off, understand that if you have taught them about their IGS, they will learn the lessons they need to learn. Your teen will learn that a lack of effort and study produces poor results. If they don't care about those results, so be it. But if they do care, they will guide themselves to allot enough study time the next time around. I know it can be challenging to let your kids find their way, make their own choices that you don't agree with, and watch them seemingly fail at times. I tried to push against behavior that I disapproved of and to guide my children to what I thought was their highest choice, but it can be a futile fight. I discovered that children of any age benefit the most when we relax and let go of trying to control their behavior and experience.

Again, by experiencing what they don't want, our kids can clearly define what they *do* want; life is not about always making the highest choice the first time around. We are here to evolve, and we accomplish this by going through what we don't want and discovering what we do. This is how we evolve, expand, and grow.

Clearly, parents can be threatened and worried about the teen years. Yet, if we have taught our children to become familiar with their IGS, and if we allow them to use it, they have a greater chance of making better choices for themselves.

So, how does this come to pass? First, our teens must know they have an IGS. Second, they must focus internally to feel the messages coming through. Then, it's time to move toward what *feels the best* or away from something that doesn't. It is the internal feeling of wanting or not wanting to do or have something that serves as one's guide. For example: A teen may choose to skip school because, at the time, other activities sound infinitely more fun. In that moment, their highest choice is to *not* attend school because not only do they want to do something else instead, but also they feel that they won't learn anything and thus won't benefit. Of course, their parent believes they *will* benefit and therefore *want* the teen to attend class.

So in terms of the Law of Attraction and the advisability of following one's IGS, will the teen's choice serve his best interest? This depends on whether or not the individual is in alignment. When your children are in alignment and feeling joyful, they are on their highest path toward all the answers they seek. It is in this state of being that they receive guidance and inspiration. Sometimes a child's joy is found doing activities that we as parents don't agree with or approve of. We have to remember, however, that a child in alignment is not going to go down a path of destruction. That would be contradictory to the laws of our Universe, **which are absolute.** Although your child may lose school credits or get suspended when he skips school, these consequences serve as a learning tool. He will have to choose whether to conform and continue attending classes, or not. What he truly wants will determine his highest choice.

The teen that truly wants to walk with his friends at graduation will get back to attending class. If he does not want to be in class, no matter the cost, he will find a way not to be. Perhaps trying to concentrate is too difficult for him, or maybe he has big dreams and passions that are pulling him forward—away from school—toward realizing those dreams right now. Richard Branson, who owns Virgin Airlines and over 200 other companies, left school at sixteen because he was dyslexic and had bigger dreams to fulfill. He knew in his heart that he could no longer be at school, but I imagine his parents thought otherwise.

It can be hard for parents to feel supportive of their child if he or she is not performing within the expected timeline—not finishing high school with the rest of his class, for example, or making the decision to drop out. But most teens have a timeline all their own. If we can acknowledge this and trust in our higher process—guiding but not controlling our kids—we will be less stressed, and so will our children as they find the way toward their best path.

USING THE HIGHER PROCESS TO GUIDE YOUR CHILD

The *higher process* comes in knowing and trusting that the Universe is on your side and on the side of your child. The *higher process* also exists when you allow your child to use her IGS with no attachment to results (on your part) and no judgment from you. And here is a key component: Your child's soul knows its highest path and will communicate it to the child through her IGS. When she is in alignment, she will always receive guidance and know what is right for her. This applies to children of all ages, as one's soul communicates to us at all times. One more bit of great news: **wellbeing abounds in the Universe**.

Of course we should have expectations of our children. We should expect them to live their best lives. We should expect them to follow their hearts. We should expect that they will know their path. We can facilitate this by teaching them about their IGS. We also should expect and support the fact that only they know their answers.

So let's say you have a son in middle school who doesn't want to be in a certain math class, but you know it is a requirement for graduation. He feels strongly about not wanting to take the class, but you don't agree with his choice. The key to this common parenting challenge is this: Consider the bigger picture. Kids don't always consider the big picture, and you can help him see it. You might ask your son, "What do you want—not just today but in the long run? Do you want to complete your requirements and move on to high school?" If he says yes, I would remind him that a decision not to take the math class would not support what he says he wants, which is to move on to high school. Then I would encourage him to get into alignment with his math class so he will be able to benefit from it. He would then have to find a way to appreciate some aspect of the class or some benefit he can glean from being in it.

Now, let's say your child says, "I don't care about high school or the math class!" This is a tough scenario, but one that can come up in many families. I would address the problem by asking some questions to try and determine the reason your son hates the class. Perhaps it's because there is a bully in the class or another situation that makes him feel uncomfortable. Or maybe he just hates math. I would encourage this child to use his IGS to consider all the aspects of the class and how each one feels to him. For example: the subject matter, the teacher, the other students in the class, the time of day when the class meets, the homework, the tests, and so on. By teaching your child how to use his IGS to check in with his feelings, you can help him find within himself the reasons for why he feels a certain way. In this particular situation, perhaps by considering what he specifically "hates" about his math class—and taking steps, or not, to address those conditions—your son could find resolution without having to leave the class.

When a particular problem at school gets to the point where it's your will against your child's, it often comes down to how much you are willing to push against the situation. Younger kids are often forced to comply because they have little recourse, but I believe that showing your child how to stay in or get back into alignment and listen to their IGS will serve their greater good.

I won't say it isn't tempting to give your kids an opinion on what they should do in any given situation. When my kids ask me for advice, they know by now what I'll say: I will gently remind them how to find their own answers. If they are under stress about a situation at school or conflicted about their educational path, I remind them how to access and trust their IGS, and to remember that their answers become clear when they are in alignment. I always want my kids to feel my support and care, but I don't want them to succumb to the ease—and the trap—of allowing me or others to decide their actions.

My college daughter once came to me to confide that she was in the throes of hating a particular class. Since it was a requirement, she didn't want to drop it. But she was having trouble changing her attitude toward the class. What should she do? I told her that she couldn't suddenly decide to love the class because that was too great an emotional stretch from hating it. What she could do was take baby steps and slowly work her way up her emotional scale, feeling better about the class and the teacher a little bit at a time. I suggested that every day while in class, she should focus on one small thing to appreciate about being there. Maybe all she could appreciate at first would be the view out the window; the next day, it might be the teacher's voice or the fact that she had friends in the class. Perhaps remembering that she usually feels better after settling into her classes would produce a more positive, appreciative feeling. Even these relatively minor appreciations would help her create an eventual appreciative energy vibration toward the class.

Why is it so important to teach your children to practice appreciation—in this instance, as it pertains to school and their education? As you practice appreciation, it becomes more a part of your experience (what you manifest), and you're given more things to appreciate by the Universe. It only takes a few seconds on a thought of appreciation before the Universe will send you back a matching thought, and in a few minutes you will be on a roll with the momentum and feeling much better. I told my daughter, "Be sure to amp up your appreciation every day, and that sense of appreciation will become what you experience. It will ultimately translate into better feelings about being in the class or anything else in your life you want to experience in a more positive way."

GIVE YOURSELF AND YOUR CHILD AN A IN IGS

In this chapter, we've explored the challenges and benefits of encouraging your children to follow their IGS as they navigate their educational path. Of course, in order to allow them to do their part, we need to do ours. As parents, we need to accept that every child has her own interests and passions and learns at her own pace. Your children aren't in school in order to accomplish our goals or those of their classmates; they are there to create and work toward their own. It will be up to them to develop the skills they need to get to where they want to go. Your children can use their Internal Guidance Systems to help them determine their desired course.

Here are some parental guidelines that I hope you'll find helpful as you support and encourage your child along the way:

- Guide your child so that she is familiar with her IGS and knows how to trust it.

- Inspire your child to enjoy learning what he wants to learn, rather than insisting that he follow your educational agenda.

- Understand that every child learns when she is ready, and allow your child to follow her own learning timeline.

- Respect your child's chosen educational path.

- Allow your child to take responsibility for his schoolwork and let go of the urge to check up on him.

- Show an authentic, focused interest in your child's schoolwork—without demanding certain grades or results.

- Help your child to have positive feelings about some aspect of school.

- Find schools that are more progressive about children charting their own course.

N O T E S

CHAPTER 5

Letting Your Kids Choose
Their Own Friends

The relationships that our children have with their friends are among the most valuable they will ever experience. Friendships help them learn how to listen and give support. They learn the give-and-take of human relationships from a place of equality by being equal to their peers and separate from the hierarchy of the family.

As you watch your children grow, you are privy to the importance that their friends hold in their lives. You have the opportunity to support them as they experience their dramas, betrayals, and joys. A parent who values closeness with their child also values their child's friends. This doesn't mean that you will always like and approve of who your child chooses as a friend. My children chose some pretty interesting characters at times. Valuing your child's friends means that you recognize that every relationship your child chooses is a gift. Every relationship benefits them in some way.

Remember that your child has his or her own IGS and will choose the friends they want to learn from on a soul level. This won't be a conscious choice, but one made from the level of their soul. Some will be positive relationships, and others will appear negative. Yet, every relationship can have value if you teach your children to be conscious of who they are, what they want, and what they are experiencing.

Children learn who they are by experiencing different aspects of themselves, and friendships bring out various facets of a child's personality—the good and the not-so-good. Kids are able to define who they want to be by experiencing the opposite of who they are, and friendships provide an excellent platform for this. Again, by experiencing what we don't want, we can clearly define what we *do* want.

We can help our children to not get stuck in friendships that don't feel good by encouraging them to stay true to themselves, identify what they want in a friend, and focus on enjoying that kind of relationship. Throughout this chapter, we'll explore how you can teach your child these important principles while still allowing them to choose their own friends.

CAN YOUNG CHILDREN BE TRUSTED TO CHOOSE THEIR OWN FRIENDS?

In a word: Yes! **Our souls know no age and have innate knowledge of our life purpose.** Children not only have access to this self-knowledge, but also they tend to be closer to it. Unlike adults, they haven't yet had the opportunity to forget. We tend to forget our life purpose as we age unless we have made a conscious choice not to, or if our focus is not particularly intense. In other words, when we are very young, we are closest to our Source, where we came from, pure positive energy, the all-knowing place of the soul that knows our purpose in this life.

Remember, each of us emits an energy vibration. This is the Law of Attraction. **Our thoughts and feelings are emitted as a vibration—a signal—and we attract whatever people, things, and experiences match this vibration.** So, it is important to trust your child to choose the friends that he or she will learn and grow from, whether the value of their friends is evident to you or not.

When your child is old enough to have a dialogue with you, you can start to teach them about using their IGS to choose their friends. You can help a young child tap into their IGS by encouraging them to ask themselves these questions:

- How do I feel when I am with my friend?

- How do I feel about myself when I am with my friend?

- How do I feel about the choices I make when I am with my friend?

- Do I do things with my friend because I really want to—or because he wants me to?

- Did I choose this friend because I like him—or because other kids think he's cool?

If your child feels good about their experience with their friend, then they are in alignment with this friendship. But what about when a friendship *doesn't* feel good, or your child can't get along with a certain friend? You can show your child that friends who are different from us give us a chance to grow and determine what we want, and can benefit us greatly. How to demonstrate this to a young child? By encouraging them to talk about what kind of friend they would like to have. You can both have fun describing the perfect friend, perhaps even writing down the qualities of a good friend.

This is also the time in a child's life when they start to discover that others don't always play by our rules, do as we want or expect them to, or invite us to their birthday parties. The latter scenario can be devastating to a child. What do we say to a young child to lessen their hurt feelings? Maybe a dialogue with your child might go something like this:

> **Your daughter**: *Sarah didn't invite me to her birthday party, and I'm sad.*
>
> **You**: *Sweetheart, people become our friends because of the feelings we have inside. Our feelings are invisible energy that touches our friends. But sometimes our feelings don't match their feelings. Your feelings don't match Sarah's right now, so maybe that's why you weren't invited.*
>
> **Your daughter**: *But I want to be her friend and go to her party.*
>
> **You**: *I know you do. And I hope her feelings match yours very soon. In the meantime, it is important to have fun and feel good. Maybe your good feelings will match the feelings of other friends.*

In addition to helping your child use her IGS to choose and assess her friendships, it's important that you find a way to feel a certain amount of peace regarding your child's friends. You can do this by using your own parental IGS. Perhaps your child has a friend who exhibits behavior that is offensive to you, but your child is adamant about maintaining the friendship. You have a choice to make. Remembering that what you focus on is brought into your experience. It's likely that you are focusing on aspects of this person that don't feel good to you, which can cause a lot of unnecessary angst. But you can choose to change your focus.

First, you can change your intention by looking for positive traits in this child that your son or daughter has chosen as a friend. Your power lies in your intention. Then, take a deep breath and trust that your child will gain clarity about this person. Unless the friend is physically abusive or is putting your child at serious risk, be open to seeing the more positive aspects of your child's chosen friend. Whatever they are looking for in a friend, they will find.

I encouraged my kids to seek friends and be around people whom they perceived as different, smarter or even more accomplished in some way. Why? **Because the higher consciousness of others will inspire one's own consciousness to rise.** What you see in another person, you can start to see in yourself. On the other hand, sometimes my children chose friends who exhibited traits that didn't seem very inspiring. Still, those friendships were of value as well because each person serves as a mirror to help us see the qualities we embody. In other words, friends show us aspects of ourselves that we love, as well as aspects that we may decide don't serve us after all.

TEACHING KIDS HOW TO RESPOND TO ANNOYING FRIENDS

Depending on your child's personality, their friendships may revolve around a lot of drama and conflict. While such scenarios can be challenging, they offer an opportunity for your child to learn how to choose their responses. Reacting to things and people almost never gets us what we want, because reaction is a negative emotional response that can leave us feeling powerless. When we are powerless, we aren't able to offer any inspiration that will lift the situation. All of us, including children, have the capacity to choose our response to another's behavior—and this allows us to remain feeling good, and in our power.

Deliberately choosing how to respond to a difficult or annoying friend begins with teaching your child to *practice observing the drama—* what is happening around them as well as what is being said. The objective is to remain detached in a way that doesn't trigger an emotional response and then to choose, consciously and deliberately, how they'll respond. This will take practice on their part, since children and teens have a tendency to be negatively reactive. But as they learn to observe their interactions with friends and to choose how they want to respond—rather than to simply react—they will learn a new awareness of themselves and others and discover their power.

None of us has control over another's behavior, and yet other people's behavior does indeed affect us. We have the highest effect on any given situation when we offer our positive thoughts, feelings, and behavior rather than reacting negatively. So our goal as parents is to guide our children to what feels best to them. For example, let's say your ten-year-old son has a friend who doesn't seem to play fair. Whenever they shoot hoops in the driveway or play a video game, the friend always seems to cheat—and deny it. Your son calls him on it, the friend denies cheating, and a fight ensues. After the friend leaves, your son comes to you complaining about his friend. What do you say?

Your son: *Jason always cheats. I can't stand him.*

You: *Well, I think you have several choices here. If you feel that Jason always cheats and that makes you feel bad, don't shoot hoops with him. Or, if you do decide to shoot hoops with him, just ignore his cheating and enjoy your time with him. If you find that you can't ignore his cheating, make the choice not to get in a fight with him. And next time, choose not to play with him.*

Your son: *So I guess it's up to me, in a way.*

You: *Right. Choose what feels best to you at the time. Since you're not having fun with him now, make some new choices. See how you feel when you're playing with him next time—and make the choice that will make you feel good.*

As my children encountered confusion in their friendships, I taught them to notice and ask themselves: *How do I feel about myself when I am with my friend?* They learned that thought is energy and that it has a vibration. One example is that when a friend is sending you loving, positive thoughts, he or she will give you a sense of wellbeing and you will feel good. On the other hand, if a friend is sending out negative thoughts and feelings about you, you will receive those vibrations and you won't feel good. There are also other scenarios that stem only from how we're feeling ourselves, regardless of how our friend is feeling.

It's also important to know that friends are a mirror for us, so what we see and feel in our friends are aspects of ourselves. And we attract from them what we send in our thoughts and feelings, which is the Law of Attraction at work. So if your child is unhappy with how a friend is treating her, encourage her to check in more closely with her own feelings.

What if your child is having a problem responding to a difficult friend? You can remind them of these essential truths that govern our friendships, regardless of how old we are:

- We have no control over our friends' behavior.

- We can observe our friends and decide if they are the kind we want to have.

- We can make the choice to be the kind of friend to others that we would like to have.

- We can observe the drama that our friend engages in and consciously choose whether we want to participate in it.

- We have the ability to choose how we react in all situations.

- We should always be aware of who we want to be in any given situation.

- We should be aware of the fact that we are in control of our own thoughts and behavior.

- Everyone is on his or her own path. We can't expect others to be a certain way in order to make us happy. **Our happiness is our own responsibility.**

- The traits we experience in another person are aspects of ourselves.

A TEEN'S IGS AND PEER PRESSURE

Every parent of a preteen or teenager knows how peer pressure can powerfully influence a child's attitudes and behavior. What I wanted for my kids was for them to eventually learn how to be more autonomous and more independent from their friends. I wanted them to appreciate their individuality and think for themselves. Kids generally want to be just like their friends. I was aware of this as I encouraged my children to become their own people. Although I was often met with resistance, I knew that once my kids learned to trust and use their IGS, they would be able to handle peer pressure and be ahead of the game as they matured into adulthood.

If they have learned how to access their Internal Guidance System, a young person will know how to check in with who they truly are and how they're really feeling—even in situations where friends may be leading them in an unwanted direction. But often the "all the other kids are doing it" scenario arises, and your teen may not be listening to his IGS. When that seems to be the case, you can steer him in the direction of his true self so that he doesn't feel obligated to cave in to peer pressure. You can remind your child to:

- Speak their own truth—express what feels good and right for them.

- Notice how they feel when they're with their friends and when they talk to their friends.

- Notice the difference between what your child is saying and how that makes them feel after they've said it.

- Observe their friends and be clear about what they are doing, what your child wants to do, and how their paths may be different.

- Notice how your child feels when they are contemplating an action their friends are engaging in.

By the time my kids reached a certain level of maturity in high school, they had learned and lived these practices long enough to have at least partially integrated them into their relationships. They began to enjoy being an example, even an inspiration, to their friends. I knew this by the stories they brought home and shared with me—about how they helped their friends feel more positive when they were experiencing an unwanted scenario. That's not to say, however, that my children always followed the path I would have chosen for them or that they only hung out with "squeaky clean" model students.

When Brittany was fifteen, she was going through a somewhat rebellious period in school—which you'll hear more about in Chapter 7. We let her live her life and be with her friends, whom we hoped would serve as a good influence. It was at this point that Brittany decided that her mainstream friends weren't right for her, and she started hanging out with some interesting new characters. None of them seemed dangerous, only different from what we were used to seeing as her friends. We started calling Brittany "the dark side of cool," and when she told me that she was considering choosing a certain boy to be her boyfriend, I reminded her in a fun-teasing manner that her self image was that of a princess. Did she think this boy would honor such an image? I encouraged her to check in with her IGS.

Her year was spent experimenting with different friendships in her quest to define herself. Even as I rolled my eyes (in private), I knew that this was an important part of Brittany's growing up and finding herself. As I mentioned earlier, kids define and fine-tune themselves by relating to others who are different from them. We come to know what we want in part by experiencing what we don't want. If we trust in this process when it comes to our teenage children, we can prevent ourselves from over-worrying. We can't control whom our kids choose as friends. We can, however, remind them to pay attention to how it feels when they are with particular friends. And we can certainly pay attention to who our kids are spending time with. I continually asked my daughters and my son pointed questions that would at least cause them to think about and evaluate their choices regarding activities and friendships. Such questions included these:

- I know that you value certain things in your life; does your friend value them as well, for themselves?

- Do you feel that your friend inspires you to be yourself—the person you truly are?

- Have you thought about how this friendship serves you right now and in the future?

BALANCING FRIEND TIME WITH FAMILY TIME

Each of my children had different needs and desires, and as they sought to establish their freedom, we experienced some challenging times. I acknowledged that it was natural for them to want to spend a lot of time with their friends, as this is an important time of growth for teens and preteens. I fully supported time with their friends, yet

I still wanted to experience our family time together, as well. So, it became all about balance. My IGS was feeling a lack of balance because my idea about family time no longer matched our family's new reality, which included less time together. So how did we create a balance?

First, I had to release my attachment to any outcome I had in mind regarding how and when this new family-friend balance would happen. I needed to let go of my expectations and "go with the flow." This meant letting my teens have their time of freedom and their time with friends, while also making my own wishes known. Your children can't be expected to know what you want; it's your responsibility to ask for it. When I began to pick up on the fact that they wanted to spend more time after school and on weekends with their friends, and that they didn't seem to value the activities we had done in the past, I realized we had to talk about this. I told them, "I understand you want to spend more time with your friends—and this is perfectly normal for kids your age. But I still want time with you, too. How can we work this out in a way that makes each of us happy?" They let me know they understood what I wanted and would try to meet my request for more family time, each in their own way and with their own parameters. Certainly this made sense to me, given that they're all such different people with varying degrees of social needs.

My kids and I had to learn the give and take of our family dynamic in which no one could have their own way entirely. I wish I could say they heartily accepted this balance of family and friend time, but that was not the case initially. I sometimes had to impose the balance by setting some ground rules. I respected their need to be with their friends, and they went along with my steadfast rule about family dinners.

I discovered that the more you show your kids that you respect their needs, wants, and fun time, the more they will trust you. By allowing them to spend enough time with their friends, you show them that you support their quest for freedom. As the years passed, my kids were able to create their own balance between family and friend time, so I no longer had to be in charge of scheduling it. And they learned to place great value on our time together, probably because I didn't force it on them.

What can family time consist of? You can cook Sunday breakfast for the family, attend church together, or go for a family outing. I tried to coordinate certain days when everyone could be together for a time. Dinner as a family, at least most days of the week, was a requirement I stuck to. Sure, there were sports and school commitments that made this challenging at times, but unless there was a special event, it was mandatory that everyone be home for a shared family dinner. I feel it's okay to lay down the law when it comes to family time because you can't really know who your kids are if you don't spend time with them. There may be periods when your kids won't say much, if anything, during shared meals, but that will eventually change as they come to integrate family time into their lives and learn to appreciate the time together.

For our family, dinner was the only time of day when I could talk to my kids during the week. The ride to school was too early for anyone to feel chatty, as they were barely awake at 6:45 a.m. when we left the house. The ride home from school was sometimes social and sometimes not, as they were tired from their day. After dinner was homework and baths, so that left dinnertime!

Over the years, the kids complained about always having to have dinner together, but in the long run this made such a difference in our family bond. The laughter and teasing warmed my heart, and even the grumpy and quiet meals where no one spoke were important, because at least we were all together. As they became teens, they insisted I not make dinner for them on Friday or Saturday nights, categorically stating, "We are not eating healthy on those nights, Mom. We want deli (fried food) from the grocery store—or we might be out with friends." Fair enough. You learn to choose your battles.

Again, the balance that's achieved between friend time and family time is important to the growth of your child and the stability of the family. Your kids need the socialization and fine-tuning of their IGS that comes with making choices related to their friendships and activities. And family time is important for the support system it offers your children and the family as a whole.

GET TO KNOW YOUR KIDS' FRIENDS

I believe in being involved with my kids' friends. In fact, some of the most fun I've experienced has been with my children's friends. I remember when my firstborn, Brittany, was little, I was still figuring out how to parent and at a complete loss as to what to say to her little friends. I simply didn't have a clue at first, and I remember being really uncomfortable. I decided the only way to learn to talk to kids is to be with them and interact with them in their space and in their comfort zones.

My children had lots of social time with their friends, playing at our house, their friends' homes, at parks, and so on. But there were also many opportunities for parental involvement, and school was one of them. All of my kids made it clear that they would be happy if I participated in their schools, so I volunteered to drive on school field trips, plan class parties, and sometimes tutor in the classroom. Being around your kids and their friends in the varied situations of their lives helps you feel the essence of their spirits, hear their laughter, and receive the love that children so generously give. It becomes easier and easier to be a comfortable part of their world and to embrace who they are.

Since I had always participated with the kids and their friends when they were younger, the transition into the teen years was smoother. It wasn't strange to have Mom on the scene, lending support. When they were teenagers but before they were able to drive, I often volunteered to drive them and their friends to various activities, which gave me the chance to get to know whom they were hanging out with. I also enjoyed having kids come to our house, and I always made sure to have lots of food on hand. Our home became the place where kids liked to get together, which was fine by me. I was relieved to know that my kids were in a safe place, and it gave me the opportunity to get to know their friends.

The names and faces have changed and all of my kids' friends are taller and more mature now, but I continue to enjoy being around them. I appreciate them as people, I love them for the relationship they have with my children, and I love talking with them and hearing about the paths they are creating. I love witnessing their drama and their joys. Being present, listening, and talking with your children's friends shows your kids that you value their choices. In other words, your children feel valued when you value their friends. It shows them that you respect and trust their choices as they use their IGS.

I believe that our kids want us to like their friends but aren't willing to let us determine which friends they should have. And that's as it should be. They should be the ones to choose, not us. Your child may have friends whom you wish they hadn't chosen, but when you can see the value in all their relationships, you're able to remove the judgment and replace it with support.

Perhaps your son has brought home a friend that you hadn't yet met. You want your son to feel that you are interested in who his friends are, so you engage with the friend and inquire about his interests and activities. Kids want to feel respected, and when we show our interest in their friends—the people whom they value— they in turn feel valued by us.

CAN YOU BE A FRIEND AND A PARENT?

Although we may long for the day when we can finally be a friend to our child and not just a parent, there is a delicate distinction between the two. It is an art to be in one role and be able to effortlessly switch to the other when circumstances dictate.

When children are young, it's easier to wear two hats at the same time. We are in parental mode as we teach them and guide them through their daily lives; being the authority figure is our natural role. You are a special adult friend to a younger child when you listen to them as they express their hopes, fears, dreams, and frustrations. Or when you get down on the floor and help them build a Lego monster.

During the teenage years, things can become more convoluted. It may seem easier to be more of a friend than a parental authority figure since setting limits and offering guidelines can be met with resistance. Rather than deciding how to deal with a rebellious teen, it can be tempting to take the easy way out and just be the friend, without trying to offer any guidance. On the other hand, even though we may have taught our children about their IGS and trust them to use it, most of us still feel the need to give guidance in certain difficult situations. But it's important to know the difference between guiding your child based upon your values and your IGS, and pushing up against and trying to control the uncontrollable.

Teens need our guidance, but not our control. Even when you don't agree with your teen's choices, you can still allow them to use their IGS. Being a caring parent means letting your child mature by allowing them to make decisions and mistakes. It also means being there with your support and guidance when necessary. While some parents try to be their teens' best friend—"one of the guys" or "one of the girls"—kids of any age feel uncomfortable and insecure when there is no real parental figure to turn to. You can offer your teen certain qualities of a good friend, like compassion, understanding, and acceptance, which may involve simply listening to them. At the same time, they appreciate your being there for them as their parent, providing them with a positive role model and a wise counselor.

At this stage of their lives, teens are discovering their autonomy and their freedom. If you can adapt to this natural order of things, offering your understanding and guidance (rather than either demanding compliance or being an adult pal), your teens will have a better chance of developing a strong sense of self. As any savvy parent knows, we have no control over our teen's actions, including their choice of friends. Our job as parents is not to control their lives, but to assist them in creating their own path and experiencing their own consequences. Your kids may make some odd, even frightening, choices when it comes to their circle of friends, but that's why it is so critical to teach them about their Internal Guidance Systems.

EVERY FRIEND IS A GIFT

Your children's friends offer them the opportunity to learn about themselves and the world, to make choices on their own, and to test the waters of human relationships. Knowing this, you can easily acknowledge that every friend—no matter how strange or unruly—is a gift.

The following guidelines summarize what we've discussed in this chapter:

- When you allow your child to choose his own friends, it enables him to clearly decide and define—on a soul level as well as a conscious level—what kind of friendship he wants.

- Every friendship benefits your child by showing her various aspects of herself, as reflected in those she connects with.

- Your child learns about himself based upon what thoughts and feelings he is vibrating and hence what type of friends he is attracting.

- You can teach your child to access her feelings about her friends by using her Internal Guidance System. This will help her to let go of friendships that don't feel good.

- Although friends who "don't feel good" are valuable in that they show your child what he *doesn't want*, his IGS can help him clarify the type of friendship he *does want*.

- When you show your child that you value her friendships, you demonstrate that you trust her to use her IGS.

- Children place great importance on their friends, so when you value your child's friends, you show that you value him.

- If your child is hanging out with less-than-desirable friends, encourage her to ask herself these powerful questions:

  ✓ How do I feel when I am with my friends?

  ✓ Do my friends reflect who I am?

  ✓ Do I share my friends' values?

  ✓ How comfortable am I with the choices I make when I am with my friends?

  ✓ Do I take pride in my friendships?

NOTES

CHAPTER 6

Allowing Kids to Develop Their Own Habits

N one of us enjoys the role of "nagging parent." After all, who relishes the unpleasant job of badgering kids to clean up their room, do their homework, or stop eating so much junk food? As parents, we don't want to be accused of trying to control our children. In fact, what we want most is for our kids to become responsible for their own lives, to do what we believe is the right thing without our having to ask them—or hound them. But how many of us get through the parenting cycle, from toddlerhood to young adulthood, without succumbing to parental nagging? "How can I *not* nag my child?" you might ask. "If I don't, he'll walk around in dirty clothes, she'll flunk out of school, and they'll eat nothing but pizza!"

As we've been discussing throughout the book, allowing a child to follow their Internal Guidance System can be quite challenging for a parent. Giving up control and letting your child decide for themselves what is "the right thing" to do so that they can deal with various issues on their own is never easy. But if you introduce your children to the principles of the Universal Law of Attraction and can hang in there as they learn to trust their IGS, you'll be pleasantly surprised by how they will benefit. They will gain the experience of testing themselves, making decisions, and figuring out on their own how best to handle life's trials.

In this chapter, we're going to address the issue of so-called bad habits. I don't actually like that phrase, because it is negative and judgmental. After all, one person's bad habit is another person's perfectly reasonable routine. And yet, many of us worry that if our children don't change a particular habit when they're young, they'll be stuck with it as an adult. But when a young person can turn to their IGS to consider whether or not a habit is worth hanging onto, rather than simply going along with what an adult demands of them, they will be that much further along on the path to maturity. As a parent, you'll find that by appropriately relinquishing control over your children, you will allow them to grow and take control of their own lives.

GIVING UP CONTROL AND GIVING IT TO YOUR CHILD

I'm not sure how Dustin and I survived his childhood. In my quest to be the perfect parent, if I sensed a flaw in his behavior or a potential problem that he wasn't adequately addressing, I thought I should jump in and help fix it. Such was the case when it came to his eating habits.

By the time Dustin was a preteen, he had been putting on weight for a few years. I made sure that I served only healthy meals and snacks, and I limited the amount of sweets in the house since they were clearly a weak point for Dustin. But when I started to hide the snacks and chips that I saved for the kids' school lunches, Dustin began looking in every nook and cranny of our house until he found what I had hidden. My attempt to prevent him from having the snacks only resulted in Dustin feeling that he couldn't have what he wanted. I had created a situation in which Dustin felt he was being deprived, which only added to his weight gain and contributed to his already poor attitude.

I decided something had to be done, so I took Dustin to a medical food clinic, where he could be taught the importance of healthy eating and food choices. We attended their sessions a few times, and although the clinic offered a good program, Dustin wanted nothing to do with it. I don't think he learned much from the program, but I sure did. This was to be *my* lesson.

Counseling sessions with a therapist were part of the program, and it was during those sessions that I had my awakening moment. As the therapist was talking about what was occurring in our home, I realized that my behavior was contributing to Dustin's poor eating habits. I was horrified. I came to see that in hiding the food, I was making him want it all the more. And I had been fooling myself that I could control Dustin's behavior. Indeed, the illusion of control had been compelling, even intoxicating.

It seems so obvious looking back that what I was doing was counterproductive, but when you are in the midst of a situation that doesn't feel good, it is hard to see the big-picture perspective. Although I couldn't see it then, I certainly did during our sessions with the therapist. As she was speaking to us, I experienced a powerful revelation regarding what I was creating.

When we got home from this particular session, Dustin and I had a heart-to-heart talk, and I agreed I would no longer hide the snacks. Instead, they would be kept in the cupboard. His part was agreeing not to abuse them by eating them all in one day. The act of relinquishing a perceived control over a situation, in which I had never actually had any control whatsoever, was one of the hardest things I have ever done. I suffered greatly thinking that Dustin would now be free to overeat and simply put on more weight.

He did, for a while. I had to remind Dustin of our agreement over and over, and at first it was torture not hiding the snacks. It was surely a process, and with time I learned to trust that Dustin could call on his Internal Guidance System to act in a way that was best for him. And he did eventually learn to recognize when he was truly hungry as opposed to eating out of boredom or frustration.

There came a time when the snacks would remain in the cupboard uneaten for long periods. Not only had Dustin benefitted from being in control of his own eating habits, but I believe that we as a family greatly benefited from this shared life experience, hard as it was sometimes.

Perhaps you're experiencing something similar in your own family. Maybe it isn't related to food issues but to another troubling behavior or perceived bad habit that your child is exhibiting. You might want to ask yourself these questions:

- Am I attempting to control my child's habits?

- How is that working out for me and for my child?

- When I check in with my IGS, how does the act of trying to control my child's behavior feel?

- How does my child likely feel when I attempt to control him?

- If I give up my control, might he be able to deal with the issue on his own?

- Have I taught my child about his IGS and worked with him so that he understands it and feels comfortable trusting it?

As you face the challenge of allowing your child to be in control of his or her own habits and routine, it is helpful to remind yourself of some of the principles of the Universal Law of Attraction. **Each of us is here in this life to create our own highest ideal.** There are no "shoulds," and there is nothing we have to accomplish or be.

We are all here to be free, to create, and to express ourselves. The joy is in the process, the constant creation of new ideas, always moving forward. There is only wellbeing that flows to each of us from the Universe, and it will always guide us toward our best choices.

We can teach our children to follow their highest impulses, and when they do, they will be in tune with their highest self—their joy. These impulses are messages intended just for them, and if we are supportive but not controlling, our children can learn to honor the messages that feel good, the ones that inspire them, and move in the direction of those messages.

SAME BEHAVIOR, DIFFERENT PERSPECTIVES

Sometimes, your child perceives what you may consider bad behavior or a bad habit quite differently. For example, you may think that forgetfulness is a sign your child is not acting responsibly, whereas he may reason that he just has a lot on his mind and can't be expected to remember all the things that *you* want him to remember. Which brings me to another Dustin story.

Before Dustin left for school one morning, we agreed that he would find a ride to his driver's education lesson, where he would be taking an hour-long drive with an instructor. I called him after school to make sure he had found a ride to driver's ed as planned.

While we were on the phone, Dustin informed me he'd forgotten his wallet, which contained his driver's permit. This meant no driver's ed that day, as they won't let him take the lesson without it. Although Dustin had taken the initiative to call his driving school and cancel, I wasn't pleased. I admit that I like things to go according to plan, and in this particular case I felt it was irresponsible of my son to have forgotten his permit. Dustin responded to my disapproval by telling me that he believed he had behaved responsibly by taking the initiative to call the instructor, and that he felt good about how he had handled the situation. His final words to me during that conversation were "Guess not"—meaning that he guessed, after hearing my displeasure, that he had *not* behaved responsibly. So even though he initially thought he had handled the situation well, my disapproval had him feeling that he *hadn't* handled it well at all. The moment I hung up the phone, I realized the mistake I had made and couldn't wait to talk with him when he got home. I later told him that I was glad he had felt good about his decision to handle the situation by informing the driver's ed teacher he couldn't make it that day. I validated the fact that he had followed his own Internal Guidance System. And I conveyed that I didn't want him to allow me to make him feel wrong.

I explained that throughout his life, there will often be someone who doesn't agree with his choices, whether it's me, friends, a girlfriend, his wife, or anyone else—and that's okay. You simply can't please everyone, but you will always make the right decision for yourself when you listen to your IGS. Although we have no control over others, the lesson here is to stay true to you. It is imperative to realize that you have made the right decision if it felt good while you made it. By *feel* good, I mean the peaceful place inside of you, which feels true and correct.

Yes, it would have been ideal if Dustin had remembered his wallet and not missed the driver's ed lesson. But the lesson for me was that he handled the situation in the way that he felt was best. And that's a good thing.

Does your child exhibit certain habits that drive you crazy? Do you have a tendency to label that behavior as bad or irresponsible or sloppy? What if you were to reconsider the behavior from your kid's perspective? Might you find it easier to give up trying to control it? Perhaps combing her hair and wearing clean clothes are not a priority for your daughter. Maybe she's more focused on trying out for the soccer team or creating her own comic strip as a creative outlet. Your son may prefer playing video games when he gets home from school instead of getting down to his homework right away. Is it possible that he needs to unwind before tackling his science project? And if he avoids his work altogether, might he learn from his avoidance? **Might that lesson be more beneficial** than a strictly enforced homework schedule?

If we want our kids to become their own people, as opposed to our clones, we have to allow them to create their own life patterns— their own way of engaging with the world. How else can they develop into authentic individuals? And if we have taught them to trust their IGS and to align with their highest selves, how can we *not* approve of the person they are in the process of becoming?

DISAPPROVAL VS. POWERFUL SUPPORT

Even if you don't actually tell your child that you disapprove of his behavior, your disapproval is apparent on a vibrational/energetic level. Our kids may *hear* us saying one thing but *feel* us saying something completely different. You may *tell* your son that he is responsible for choosing his own study schedule, while at the same time sending a negative energy vibration when he spends the night before a math test shooting hoops in the backyard.

It's challenging for your children to feel your love when you're sending out contradictory vibrations, which means you aren't in alignment. One vibration is your love, the highest vibration in the Universe; the other vibration contains the negative thoughts about your child's behavior. So your child feels love on the one hand and disapproval on the other. When this is the case, it can be hard for him not only to feel your trust and love, but also to trust his own IGS. In the above scenario, the young man might be thinking, "Mom told me I could study according to my own time frame, but she's obviously upset that I'm not studying right this minute. So I guess I'm not doing the right thing."

On an energetic level, your child will not feel the pure power of your love and support when there is a contradictory vibration, meaning contradictory thoughts. In order to have a positive influence on your child (or on anyone else, for that matter), you must be in alignment. Your power rests in your alignment. But when you are expressing discomfort and disapproval of your child, you can't help but be out of alignment.

What does it mean to be in alignment with respect to your role as a parent? It means that when you are with your children, you see the best in them and expect the best from them. It means that your thoughts match your actions and desires for them. Again, your energetic vibration will be more powerful than anything you say or do. The energetic level is the powerful place of our higher selves, of the Universe. Children will be more profoundly affected by the vibration (energy) that they feel in any given experience than by anything else.

It's immensely valuable for children to feel that your love is authentic and originates from the deepest place. They can sense that you aren't in alignment if you are *acting* loving, but not *feeling* loving. I felt very transparent at times because my kids could always see through me and called me on it when my words didn't match what I really felt. When I felt the discrepancy between my words and what I knew I was giving off in my energy, I would leave the room for as long as it took to feel better. This way I would have a greater influence on my children, and they wouldn't experience the dissonance in my energy.

Children are wonderful teachers and can keep us accountable. I remember having a hard time with a particular lesson that my kids brought to my attention. It involved a seemingly insignificant habit, but one that most parents confront at some point: the messy room. I had taught my kids to trust their IGS and establish their own routines, reminding them often that *they were in charge* of deciding when to do their homework, how early they needed to get up for school, and how they wanted to maintain their bedrooms (messy or neat). Still, there were times when I would walk into my daughters' or son's room and ... flip out! How could they live in such chaos? Even when I didn't say a word, my disapproval was obvious. My vibration would communicate my displeasure, and the child with the messy room in question would respond, "What? What's the matter, Mom?" It was clear to my kids that I was contradicting what I had taught them: that I trust them to manage their routines and habits.

So how did I turn around the situation so that it felt good to everyone involved? I made the decision to stop pushing against the untidy room scenario because I couldn't change it, and it didn't feel good to argue about it continually for years on end. I realized how wasteful it was to argue over the cleanliness of a bedroom when it never stayed clean very long when I made them clean it up, anyway. My frustration turned into a renewed commitment to trust my kids. I chose to trust that they would eventually become tidy ... or not. It would be up to them. I transformed my vibration from disapproval to love and trust, and my kids felt that shift. They "got" that I had relinquished my judgment regarding the state of their bedrooms— and that I had placed the management of their housekeeping habits into the proper hands: theirs.

When our kids' habits upset us and we find ourselves projecting disapproval or anger, we need to find a way to change our vibration. There is no right or wrong way to do this. In the example I just gave, in order to change my vibration I did something that was incredibly simple: I closed the doors to my children's bedrooms and didn't go in. Sounds simplistic, but it worked for me. Over time, thanks to the "closed door policy," I no longer had a negative reaction to their messy rooms, and the bedroom issue faded from importance.

Postscript: I hoped that my kids eventually would tire of messiness and learn that order in all things gives one a sense of wellbeing and peace. Now that they have matured, two of my three kids have indeed found this concept to be true!

Does your child have certain habits that drive you wild? Do you find yourself wasting time and energy and sacrificing good feelings wishing that she would stop doing things her way and start doing things in a way that would make you feel more comfortable? If so, think about what your wish actually means. You want them to change to be more like you, and you want them to do so according to your timetable. Even if you are paying lip service to giving them the freedom to do things their way, your disapproving thoughts and feelings will get through to them and may undermine their confidence in their Internal Guidance System.

So why not take steps to see that your child's habits don't bother you so much? It may involve something as simple as closing the door to a messy room. Understand that your child is working out how to get along in the world—using her own routines and habits. And when you offer the vibration that says "I trust you and love you," they will gain the confidence they need to progress. Isn't that an outcome you'd strongly approve of?

HABITS WITH SERIOUS CONSEQUENCES

Habitually letting your bedroom deteriorate into a state of chaos is one thing; long-term habits that don't serve you are quite another. At one point my daughter Raven was unwittingly charting a less-than-healthy course due to her tendency to attract drama into her life. Again, children learn from what they experience, and Raven's experience of habitually swinging from life's highs to its lows landed her in the hospital before she was able to acknowledge the lesson that presented itself.

Raven's momentum through life has always been swift, and she was a joy to watch as she energetically moved through her experiences. As she grew up, things had a tendency to be either really good or really bad. When she was younger, she moved so rapidly through every experience that she tended to either succeed or crash dramatically. While pulling an all-nighter during her sophomore year in college, she experienced severe stomach pains and decided to treat her symptoms with over-the-counter meds. Never dreaming it could be anything serious, she went to bed in excruciating pain. In the middle of the night, she was in such agony that her roommate drove her to the emergency room. It turned out that Raven needed immediate surgery for appendicitis.

I arrived several hours after she had awakened from surgery. Having just gotten off the airplane, I walked into her hospital room to see it was filled with friends and flowers. Raven was her happy self, laughing heartily. She gave me a big hug and said she was so glad I was there. She was sore, but the situation had not been critical and her operation was a success.

Over the next two days, Raven snuggled under a blanket on the couch while I happily cooked for her and her girlfriends. For me, this was heaven—I was having quiet, quality time with my nineteen-year-old! On the third day after her surgery, Raven was ready to leave her apartment, so we went out to breakfast. Our conversation enabled her to have an enlightening moment. Because we'd already had a lifetime of my teaching her the Law of Attraction, I decided to jump right in. Here is the gist of our conversation:

> *"Well, dear daughter, as you know, everything that comes into your experience matches the vibration that you have been putting out. You have attracted a physical condition by being in a resistant state for a long enough period of time to manifest this."*
>
> *"But Mom, I am such a happy person!"*

*"That may be true, but there is more at play here. I see
the high drama with which you experience your friendships,
and I notice that you often tell me of being upset with one
of your girlfriends, or that everyone is mad at so-and-so.
For quite a while now I have witnessed your crises involving
intense drama and negative emotion, and I believe that they
have manifested into your current state of health."*

Raven had no retort. She looked at me pensively and nodded
her head. What I was suggesting—that she had a habit of attracting
chaos and drama into her life—was sinking in. Having experienced
the trauma of a painful episode and an emergency surgery, and being
nudged into acknowledging that her habits had likely attracted her
state of ill health, Raven was willing to own the truth. The Law
of Attraction had been proven once again. The high drama in her
friendships could have indeed attracted her recent health crisis.

Raven realized that she had the power to change her habits of
thought—including those that can result in serious consequences. And
she knew that she could use that power, her IGS, to attract a healthier
life. She started to choose more closely the direction her thoughts
took her and to refocus when drama was threatening her wellbeing.
This took practice, attention, and an eventual intention to become the
observer of drama and not the front-and-center participant. Ever since
her hospital episode and over time, she's done it quite successfully.

OFFERING KIDS IGS TOOLS TO ASSESS THEIR HABITS

The beautiful thing about teaching your children about the
Universal Law of Attraction is that they can use this wisdom to
create the life they envision for themselves. Part of this creative
process involves creating and testing the routines and patterns that
feel right to them. Kids experiment with various habits and behavior

throughout childhood and beyond, and it's this experimentation, when weighed against the teachings of their IGS, that will help them grow. So rather than trying to control when your kid does her homework, how much food he eats, or how many extracurricular activities she signs up for, why not focus on offering your children these IGS tools so that they can assess their habits and figure out if what they are engaged in is contributing to what they really want for themselves? Remind them to:

- Think about what you intend for your life. Ask yourself, "What kind of life do I want to create?"

- Make lists of what you want. Talk about what you want with your family and friends. Consider all the wonderful possibilities.

- *Feel* what it would be like to have what you really want. Experience this good feeling over and over. How would you act if you had what you wanted?

- Practice feeling the joy of being the person you want to be. Do this often, and talk about it often. Close your eyes, relax your body, and feel it. Focus on the feeling and on knowing that you are what you want to be and have what you desire. Have faith in your choices and allow no doubts to enter your mind. You are creating your life in every moment, so consciously choose what you want and make it happen.

- Understand that when you choose something you *don't* want over and over again, you will wonder why you're unsatisfied.

- Think about how your behavior and your routines contribute to what you really want. Observe what you are creating by engaging in those habits. If it's different than your highest vision, think about changing your focus, turning your attention away from what you don't want, and putting all your energy into what you do want.

NOTES

CHAPTER 7

Trusting Your Teen's Inner Guidance System

According to the National Institute of Mental Health, recent studies on brain development may help to explain some of our teens' risky behavior:

> One interpretation of all these findings is that in teens, the parts of the brain involved in emotional responses are fully online, or even more active than in adults, while the parts of the brain involved in keeping emotional, impulsive responses in check are still reaching maturity. Such a changing balance might provide clues to a youthful appetite for novelty, and a tendency to act on impulse—without regard for risk.[1] "The Teen Brain: Still Under Construction," National Institute of Mental Health, NIH Publication No. 11-4929, 2011.

---

[1] http://www.nimh.nih.gov/health/publications/the-teen-brain-still-under-construction/a-spectrum-of-change.shtml

So, the question for parents is this: Can we trust our teenage kids to follow their Inner Guidance Systems, which are based on their highest motivations? Or will their IGS be undermined by their normal, yet still developing, brains?

In this chapter, I would like to share several stories that reveal the challenges I faced with my daughters as they were navigating the choppy waters of their teen years. I'll admit that my faith in their IGS was profoundly tested, but these experiences ultimately fortified my belief that each of us deserves the opportunity to follow our Internal Guidance System—or not. I came to understand that teens must be free to take risks, despite their rebellious tendencies and our parental fears, in order to learn the lessons they need to learn.

SCHOOL IS NOT IMPORTANT TO ME: BRITTANY'S STORY

Brittany, my oldest, had always been a calm, fun, "together" child. I remember looking at her at age five and thinking, "This small person is so okay with who she is." She seemed to have such a strong sense of self. She had been an easy baby, and always a delight. She seemed to like to please others. As a Gemini sign, being mellow and easygoing came easily to Brittany. From my perspective, her elementary and middle school years passed fairly joyfully.

Her four middle school years had been spent at an all-girls school, and when Brittany voiced her desire to have a "real" high school experience, I agreed. Soon she was in a coed environment, surrounded by 1,200 students. She was very excited to be in a public school … with boys.

In high school, gone were the days of one-on-one nurturing by the teachers, when each girl was made to feel special. Gone, too, was the role I would play as an on-the-school-scene parent. During Brittany's pre-high school days, I had always been involved in class field trips and parties and had enjoyed listening to the girls' chatter in the car as we went from one fun activity to another. I anticipated carrying on this level of participation once Brittany was in high school and was certain that field trips remained in my future. Wrong. I discovered that parents don't drive on field trips in high school; the kids are bussed. No worries, it would still be fun being with Brittany and all her friends. On one occasion, a cavalcade of buses was called in to take all 300 freshmen to the symphony, and I was assigned to a bus that Brittany wasn't even on. Not only did I not know a single child on my bus, but the closest I came to interacting with Brittany on that symphony field trip was a quick wave across the auditorium. The days of being a class parent were over. I was learning that Brittany was on her own—in more ways than one.

It didn't take long before Brittany decided she didn't really want to participate in school. She went to her classes, but did not do the work—a horror for any parent. How many times had we told her that her high school GPA really counts and that she would need to apply herself to her studies? Early into the semester, Brittany's ambivalence became increasingly apparent to me, so I did what any good parent might do: I called the principal and cried, "Help!" This was my first child in high school, and I didn't know what to do with a noncompliant kid. The principal was wonderful and immediately called a meeting with Brittany, most of her teachers, her father, and me. It was a support conference to offer Brittany whatever help she might need to succeed in high school. I was hoping that the conference would help her, but I noticed she had a neutral expression on her face throughout the meeting. I felt helpless. I can only imagine how terrifying it must have actually felt for Brittany to be confronted by so many authority figures.

I wish I could say that our daughter immediately came around and all was well, but it wasn't. Brittany became increasingly less involved with school, doing the minimum amount of work so as not to actually flunk out. In those days, and especially with our firstborn, our parental reactions could be harsh. Brittany's father and I believed that by taking away something of value, she would be spurred into complying with homework and schoolwork. In this case, the "something of value" would be her freedom; she would be forced to come home after school and miss out on her social activities. It didn't take us long to realize that Brittany was perfectly happy being at home. She spent most of the school year coming straight home and writing poetry and songs in her room. She showed no signs of rebellion and actually didn't seem to mind her "home detention."

By her sophomore year, we were praying for improved grades. At fifteen, Brittany's attitude was not an issue. In fact, during the two years when she was distancing herself from school, she remained her delightful, loving self. I continued to remind Brittany of her IGS and that ultimately it was up to her to decide what was important to her. It took me a while to surrender to the fact that she was indeed following her IGS, that she was perfectly happy with her current situation, and that all was well with her. It was I who was pushing against the issue. Brittany simply didn't want to do much schoolwork. When a school year of home detention failed to produce better grades, we decided that grounding her was a complete waste of time. Nothing grand had been accomplished. So we let her see her friends again. Because I love my daughter and this situation reminded me of what I already knew, I came to trust that she would figure this out and her life wouldn't end up in ruins.

The summer before her junior year, Brittany fell in love with a smart, boy-next-door mainstream kid who got good grades and was popular. This relationship was the catalyst that helped her define more clearly who she wanted to be. She had matured by this time and was ready to make different choices, including the choice to apply herself in school. Brittany came to these decisions on her own, knowing that they were in her best interest, based on what she currently wanted. Her junior and senior years were academically and socially very successful and fun for her as she continued her relationship with this young man and more definitively honed in on who she wanted to become.

RUNNING AWAY: RAVEN'S STORY

Being a good parent isn't all about how you guide your kids. It's about being secure in your parenting, following your own Internal Guidance System, and stepping back from a situation when you need to so that your kids can use their own IGS. It is also about knowing you have done your best even when your children are being disrespectful or completely disagree with you.

I had the opportunity to test this when Raven ran away from home at the age of sixteen. Before I tell you about her experience, let me give you a little background. I consider myself to be an emotionally available parent. I always let my kids know that I was there for them to lend support and guidance. I spent a lot of one-on-one time with each child and provided them with a childhood full of love, fun activities, and trips. I did all of this because it brought me so much joy, and I dearly loved my children. I never thought I was a particularly strict parent, though I did my best to know where my kids were when they weren't at home. If they were going to a sleepover, I called the parents of the home they were going to, introduced myself if I hadn't met them, and confirmed that it was okay with them that my daughter was sleeping over. If my girls were going to be out overnight, I felt that doing this was good parenting. Most of the moms in their friends' group did the same. I routinely discussed the dangers of drug use with my children and didn't let them ride in other teens' cars before they were sixteen. I felt that these things were the minimum I could do to try and ensure their safety and wellbeing. (Although, truth be told, we actually have no real control over our kids' actions.)

So how did it happen that one of my kids ran away from home? Raven is my middle child, born with a special joy for life and a fabulous head of auburn hair. Her fiery and independent personality was obvious to us at a very young age. Joyful and outspoken, Raven always knew what she wanted. She loved being active and earning her own money, so she insisted on working at an early age. Ever since she was thirteen, she had a job of one type or another. So when she decided to spread her wings at sixteen, it should have come as no surprise. But the manner in which she chose to fly definitely shook up our family.

I never would have predicted that Raven would run away. I thought all was well in our world. I believed that whatever discord existed between Raven and me (and her father) was par for the course for a normal teenager who craved more freedom than she was allowed to have. But Raven's quest for freedom was expressed on a much greater scale than I could have imagined. It all came to a head during a weekend when my husband (Raven's stepfather) and I were out of town. Raven threw a party at our house, I found out, and the argument that followed on the day we came home was the straw that broke the camel's back.

When I walked into the house, Raven was in the kitchen at the stove, making brunch. It was Mother's Day, so I thought, "What a nice surprise." We had been out of town for the weekend, and the kids had arrived back home after spending a couple of days at their dad's house. But I immediately sensed something was not as it should be. The look on Raven's face confirmed this, and a feeling of discomfort came over me.

As I walked around the house, I noticed things were not as I had left them, but the disarray was very subtle. The housekeeper had been the last one at the house on Friday, and the kids had not been home long enough to get things out of place. And yet, the pillows had been sat on in the living room, a space in our house that none of us uses. And up in the guest bedroom, there were tennis shoe imprints of all different sizes on the white carpet. It dawned on me that there had been a party at my house over the weekend. Although nothing had been destroyed, someone had stolen Dustin's Xbox. It felt like a terrible violation.

I then realized that the look I had seen on Raven's face was clearly related to this event. She became angry and defensive as I confronted her with my shock and distress over what I felt was a great transgression. She was very aware of the pride I took in my home, and it felt terrible to think of unsupervised teenagers in my home drinking and having access to all of my things.

My first thought was to take away something Raven valued as an initial consequence of her deceitfulness and disobedience of family rules, so I demanded she give me her cell phone. She stormed off to her room, and I was left to consider my next move. When I went into her room, she was packing a bag and said she was leaving. She was very angry and said she hated me. Though the wild look in her eyes concerned me, I forbade her to leave. I demanded that she stop such ridiculous talk about leaving and go to bed, as she had school the next day. We would discuss it all tomorrow. This would give me time to ease the shock I felt and decide how to handle her behavior. But I never got the chance.

When I checked on her early Monday morning to make sure she was getting up for school, Raven was gone. She had squeezed through a small window in the kitchen. It was evident that the window's metal bar had been broken. I had a helpless feeling of terror knowing that my sixteen-year-old daughter was out in the world and I didn't know where. In that moment, it seemed that everything I had ever done to try to ensure my children's safety had been a waste. When I calmed down enough to harbor a small rational thought, I knew I trusted that Raven had a strong sense of self and valued herself enough to make sure she would be fine and stay out of harm's way. I prayed that was so, and it brought me some much-needed comfort.

I also remembered that I had her cell phone locked in my safe, so I would have limited access to her—not that she would have answered it, knowing it was me. Then it occurred to me that I could communicate through her best friend, at whose home I thought Raven might take refuge. I called her friend's mom, and she confirmed that Raven was there. I told her that Raven's father and I would be over to pick her up, but by the time we got there, Raven was gone. She had found out that we were on our way. I later learned that we had passed her in our car as she sped away from her friend's home, unnoticed by us in a car we didn't recognize. *What to do now?* was all we could think of through our panic.

The police suggested that we register Raven on the national runaway registry, which until then I'd never heard of, let alone needed. I was advised that if she was arrested, or worse, she would be identified as a runaway and appropriate action would be taken. *This can't be happening,* I thought.

I called my best girlfriend to tell her the lengths to which I'd gone—calling the police, registering my child. Keeping in mind that my friend was raising her children with love and support, her answer was unexpected. She responded by telling me that Child Protective Services had just visited her home because her teenage daughter had attacked her the previous night and a terrible fight had ensued. We both immediately felt as if we were in a bad movie, and the shock and horror we were each experiencing expressed itself in one of the biggest fits of laughter we ever had. We sat on the phone with each other and laughed hysterically for ten minutes. The absurdity of what we each were going through with our teenage daughters had taken its toll, and the relief we felt in sharing our experiences was palpable.

Since I am a woman of action, my children's father and I lost no time and immediately kicked into high gear. I called the high school to see if Raven had come to school that day, and thankfully she had. Our search was over, but we still needed support. I contacted Raven's school counselor, who arranged a meeting with her, the vice principal, and us. During the meeting, the school officials listed our options and made suggestions. We started to feel hopeful.

A plan was hatched for the counselor to send for Raven during her next class, as she would be unsuspecting and come to the office as summoned. Then we could have our discussion and take our daughter home. It felt like a covert operation, but the plan was not to be. We were unaware of the communication network among high school friends. In the two minutes it had taken Raven's dad and me to walk to the counselor's office, we had been spotted. A friend of Raven's had seen us and told her we were on campus, giving Raven ample time to leave the building. This was now a cat-and-mouse game. We left the school feeling awful.

After I registered Raven on the national runaway list, I was assigned a police officer that contacted me by phone. Although we never met in person, he became my guiding angel. He was such a compassionate soul and gave me his private cell number, which seemed far and above normal protocol. He told me to call him for any reason regarding Raven. If I decided I wanted her to be picked up at school, he would personally see to it and bring her home. Over the next ten days, he was of immeasurable support.

By this time, it felt like we had been on a wild goose chase, with Raven always a step ahead of us. Since it had only been two days since she had left home, I told the officer that we were going to let Raven stay with her friends, which was obviously what she intended to do. If we brought her home before she was ready, she would more than likely leave again. That evening, Raven called home, somewhat angrily exclaiming that she was checking in. Imagine that—probably one of the only runaways in history who calls to check in. I told her that as long as she gave me the phone number where she was spending her nights, I would not send the police to get her at school. She agreed.

Raven was away from us for a total of ten days, and during that time she called home every few days to check in. Each time she gave me a new contact telephone number, I recognized that she was with her closest friends. Every day I called the high school attendance office to make sure she was in school, and I covertly called her job as well.

During one of her calls home, Raven angrily told me that this current situation was not about her dad or me; it was about her wanting to have a certain freedom we wouldn't allow her to have. I responded to her from the depths of my parenting experience: "Yes, it is about you!" I reminded my daughter that I knew who I was and who I had been as her parent. I had always been loving and a very present, emotionally available parent. I made it clear to Raven that I was letting her take responsibility for what was happening. And I thanked her for not blaming us for her running away.

Raven was angry that we had taken away her cell phone in response to her having thrown a party at the house when we weren't there. She was angry that she did not have the freedom she wanted. But she wasn't blaming us. By acknowledging that this episode was "about her," Raven was taking responsibility for her actions. She wasn't blaming us for our rules and the consequences we had put into place; she was expressing her need to have more independence. She needed to be away from home to test the waters.

Even though those ten days were very difficult for me, I felt a strange sense of peace for several reasons. First, knowing that Raven was at school and at work and knowing where she was spending her nights was a relief. On a deeper level, I knew that as long as she remained feeling good, Raven would follow her IGS to keep her safe and make the best decisions. I knew this because I had witnessed her maneuvering through life in the past. She had always shown me that she was going to do what felt good to her, no matter what anyone said, so I knew this faith in her own judgment and her strong sense of self and self-love would guide her properly. And I recognized that there was a higher purpose to this incident, from which we would all benefit eventually.

That higher purpose included my parental challenge: allowing Raven to go through her process of seeking independence. Clearly, her running away from home took me out of my comfort zone, but by choosing not to send the police after her and letting the scenario play out, I had allowed my daughter to figure out what she was rebelling against and what she was searching for. The incident also gave me the opportunity to have faith, even when I had no idea of the final outcome. I experienced an expansion of love for my child and in general that I would otherwise never have anticipated. In a situation that didn't feel good and that involved someone I loved very much, I had to find a deeper place of love in order to accept and trust that all was well and that nothing had actually gone wrong.

I will always remember this period as one of the great gifts of my life. My heart swells and I feel a surge of intense love when I remember this event. I learned about forgiveness at the deepest core, and perhaps it is only possible to forgive your child at such a level. Initially, Raven's running away had felt hurtful and foreign to me, and I didn't know what to do with those feelings. And yet, while she was still away from home, whatever deep violation I felt had been done to me was transformed into love and forgiveness toward her. I was astounded that my forgiveness happened so quickly and naturally, requiring no thought or effort. It just was. I forgave Raven for having a big party in my home where something was stolen; for running away, which felt like a rejection; and for the mean and disrespectful words she used. Working through this process gave me a sense of peace that helped me through those ten days.

When Raven came home, we sat down on the couch for a talk. I didn't feel very pleased with her, but I was so thankful she was there. I asked her about her time away and how she had managed with no car, cell phone, or ride to and from work and school. She explained that although she struggled at times to make deadlines and meet her responsibilities, she did the best she could and found pride and strength in her independence. *Okay,* I thought. *Well done, Raves.*

Still, I felt strongly that Raven's decision to have a party in our home while I was gone did not originate from her highest self. Did Raven use her IGS in a way that served her when she decided to have the party? No. Because when you take action when you feel negative emotion, your end result will not be a manifestation of what you want. Raven's negative emotions were feeling disrespectful toward and unhappy with her parents. In order to manifest what you want, you must feel positive emotion, and only then will you have access to your highest wisdom and best choices. If Raven had been in a joyful state of mind, she wouldn't have acted in a way that brought negative consequences. Being in a joyful space will only give you access to what serves you, those things that enhance you. This doesn't mean that what Raven manifested had no value—quite the contrary, because there is always value in negative emotion and consequences. We can clearly decide and define what we want by creating and experiencing what we don't want.

Since that incident, I have never told Raven that she did anything wrong by running away. She has a special spirit within her, and I was always conscious of keeping that alive, even when things weren't going well between us. I had to stay true to what I had spent her life teaching her, which was how to follow her IGS even when others don't agree with her. **So often as parents, we are learning the lessons we're trying to teach our kids, right along with them.**

There was, of course, a healing period that took some time; our relationship didn't improve overnight. We had to find the balance between the freedom Raven wanted and the responsibility I felt in being a good parent. When we differed over how much freedom Raven should be allowed, we had to negotiate an outcome. We both made an effort to see each other's point of view and to discuss any issue that came up. We recognized the need for compromise in order to keep the peace between us and within the family.

As I mentioned earlier, adhering to our parenting ethics is very important. Each of us wants to raise our children based on our particular values and beliefs, and we often set limits because we believe that our rules will keep our kids safe. Parenting is relatively easy until our child rebels against those rules or beliefs. Of course, their inclination to go against what we think is right is perfectly normal. They are trying to figure out for themselves how they want to live their lives. When children start wanting to make their own decisions and find their own way—and that process begins very early on—that is the time to teach them to know their IGS so they can make their best choices in a conscious way. As their parents, we don't know their highest choice, but it is our job to teach our kids how to use their Internal Guidance Systems so that they can make their own wise choices and flourish.

MAKING THE TRANSITION FROM WORRYING ABOUT YOUR TEEN TO TRUSTING HER

Perhaps you're having a hard time trusting your teen with such major challenges as being home alone over the weekend or going on a camping trip without adult supervision. Granted, these may not be privileges you are ready to grant your son or daughter until they reach a certain age. And, of course, teens' emotional maturity can vary considerably. You may worry less about your emotionally mature fourteen-year-old than your emotionally immature eighteen-year-old.

While you're waiting for maturity to fully kick in, why not practice trusting your son or daughter on a smaller scale? Remember that when they follow their IGS, they will likely choose the path that will best serve them. And it will be good practice for your teen, as well; she'll gain the experience of knowing that her parent trusts her to be in charge.

Here are some ways you might begin making the transition from worrying about your teen to trusting her:

- Let your teen have a party in your home and agree that you will stay in your room all evening. Offer a few basic rules that you'd like her to follow, but allow her to be in charge of the party.

- Allow your teen to shop for his clothes on his own. Give him a budget, but also the freedom to make his own choices. And don't judge him for his selections.

- Let your teen choose which movies she wants to see with her friends. Giving her the leeway to make these choices lets her know that you trust her to follow her interests and curiosity.

- Put your teen in charge of planning the menu and making dinner at home on occasion. Let him make the choices— without any restrictions.

TEENS COACHING TEENS

As the years went by, my kids amassed quite a bit of knowledge about the Law of Attraction, learning to have positive expectations and to deliberately create their lives. They didn't always welcome my teachings and reminders, however. At one time or another, each of them said they didn't want to hear about "creating consciously," being "accountable for their manifestations," or anything else about the Law of Attraction. Sometimes they wanted nothing whatsoever to do with the truths I had shared with them, which at first horrified me until I calmed down and remembered that kids (and many adults for that matter) don't always like to be held accountable.

Over time, my reward came when I started to see how my teachings were becoming integrated in the kids' outlook and behavior. Although words alone don't teach, their life experience and the things they were creating were validating my input. They started to see how they were in control of the lives they were creating. They also became more aware of the drama some of their friends created and how this drama didn't produce the results they wanted. My kids began telling me about how they were helping their friends become aware of how and when they were being negative, by noticing what their friends were saying and doing. In other words, I realized that my children were becoming part-time life coaches for their friends, introducing them to the core principles of the Law of Attraction and creating what they wanted through positivity.

When Dustin, my mellow and wise son, was a sophomore in high school, for example, he came home and told me of his frustration with a certain friend of his. "Mom," he said, "I was coaching Erica all day. She is so negative. I have been trying to get her to think more positively, to think about what she wants, and it is frustrating that her mood doesn't improve." I loved hearing that story, but I reminded my son that each of us is in charge of our own happiness and that he would be a greater influence on Erica with his own happiness. It was nice that he wanted to help her, but as soon as he had an end result in mind, such as her mood improving, his own vibration and mood would lower and he would not be an inspiration to her. I complimented him on being willing to share with his friends the positivity he had come to believe and live.

As for Brittany, she has always been a teacher to others, usually by example, and she has shared many of her peer coaching stories with me. One example that stands out is when my husband and I were visiting a foreign country that had experienced a major earthquake. Telephone service was down, so I wasn't able to phone the kids to tell them we were safe. When they had yet to hear from us, Raven went into a reactive panic mode. "What should we do?" she cried out to her sister. "I feel so helpless!" Without missing a beat, Brittany took a moment to center herself. She told her sister, "First, turn off the television. It is making you feel worse. Then, remember what you know: Mom is fine. Nothing bad is going to happen to her. You know she will call you as soon as she can. Your worry will work against you, so find something else to do—something fun that will distract you."

As she has matured, Brittany has incorporated my teachings into her life. On occasion, she has even become *my* coach. She reminds me of what I have taught her about following your IGS and using the Universal Law of Attraction, especially when I stumble and do or say something foolish. In fact, my kids never let me get away with anything when it comes to forgetting what I have taught them. In those instances, the tables turn, and they coach me!

Raven is also a leader and teacher, and it has made me proud to watch her coaching others while also being open to learning. One time, when she was away at college, I was giving her some of my positive coaching advice over the phone to help her deal with a situation that had come up. As I was rambling on, I stopped suddenly and said, "You may want to put this on an index card where you can see it." "Done." she said. "It's already on a sticky on my mirror." She wanted to have it handy to share with her friends. Love it!

It's gratifying to know that your kids have not only learned from you what you hoped they would, but that they have passed along the wisdom to their friends and others whom they care about. As parents, we have a tendency to forget that our kids learn from us every moment of every day, much more often through our actions than our words—and certainly from what they feel from us. When we notice that their actions and attitudes reflect the deeply held values we have tried to embody, it makes us feel very grateful. And witnessing as they coach their friends can't help but make us feel proud.

LESSONS FOR TEENS AND THE PARENTS WHO LOVE THEM

Once you and your teen are on the same page in terms of acknowledging the Universal Law of Attraction and trusting your IGS, your relationship will likely become much more relaxed. **There will always be areas of conflict, and your teens' unpredictable behavior will still concern, and even exasperate, you at times.** But if you've done your job and instilled in them a respect for their Internal Guidance System, trusting them to learn the lessons they need to learn will become easier.

Here are some general guidelines that you can pass along to your teenagers:

- My words don't teach. You will learn through your own life experience. You have the tools.

- You can only manifest your desires and create your best life when you are in alignment and feeling good.

- In each and every thought or action, ask yourself: Am I approaching this from fear or love?

- Your life experiences will help you decide who you want to be.

- You decide the meaning of your life alone. As you experience life, decide what meaning you want to give to each situation and person that comes your way. Let go of what others or society has told you the meaning should be.

- You are here to create your grandest dreams and your highest self. Feel free to change your mind, make new choices, and create yourself anew continually.

- The Universe speaks to you through your highest thoughts and feelings. Listen to them; they are your messages.

- Accept responsibility for your manifestations and everything you create. Change your mind, your focus, and your thoughts if what you create is not wanted.

- Create what you want to manifest. Don't look for them or wait *impatiently* for them. Allow them to come to you by eagerly anticipating them.

- You are here on your own unique path.

- Allow others to be on their own unique path, free from your judgment.

- Move toward what you love doing. It will always be your highest choice.

- Intention is everything. Intend what you want for your day, your week, and your life.

- Acknowledge that you are loved, you are safe, and all is well.

N O T E S

CHAPTER 8

Internal Guidance and Divorce

O ne of the most important prerequisites for a child's healthy development is growing up in a family where parents value and respect one another. This is crucial regardless of whether or not the parents still live in the same household. When there is a lack of respect between parents, a child's emotional growth may be compromised. Disrespect and mistreatment between adults can occur between parents married to one another, parents who are divorced, or between a parent and a stepparent. Of course, every set of parents has its own unique interpersonal dynamic, and children can't help but pick up on how the adults in their family relate to each other. Children learn what they live. By watching and hearing their parents interact, they learn about how to treat other people, how to handle differences, and how to show love. And certainly children are influenced in their future love relationships by what they experience at home.

I always wanted to show my kids what a functional relationship looked like, and I wanted them to understand that every relationship is always evolving, including their parents'. It's natural to have conflict in a marriage, and children need to see that there can be healthy resolution to conflict. I think it's very important, for example, that kids learn from their parents how arguments can be used as a tool to better understand the other person.

Even when their father and I made the decision to divorce, I wanted my children to see that we could still listen to each other and respect our differences. Certainly divorce is never easy for kids, but I tried to teach my children that their parents' relationship is an ongoing process and that their father and I could still treat each other with love and respect.

In this chapter, we're going to explore how your Internal Guidance System can help you make decisions regarding divorce, how your child's IGS can help them deal with your divorce, and what you can do if you are a divorced or divorcing parent to facilitate those processes.

I NEVER THOUGHT IT WOULD HAPPEN TO ME

I never thought I would get a divorce. I believed in the fairy tale, the happily ever after. When my husband and I split up, our kids were four, seven, and ten. I had been with their father since I was fifteen years old and married him at the age of twenty-three.

My children's happiness had always been at the center of my existence; they were my priority and my almost constant focus. I believed that a divorce would hurt them. Although there was no negativity or fighting in our marriage, over the sixteen years we were married, the children's father and I had gradually slipped into a pattern of living parallel lives, doing our own separate things. I loved him, but no longer in the manner that was necessary for a happy home. I came to realize that even the pain of a divorce would provide our kids with important lessons in love and in life.

I believe we follow our hearts to find our own truth, not the truth of others, which is why I felt that I needed the divorce. My heart was telling me that it was for the best.

Others ultimately benefit when we follow our own Internal Guidance System and discover our own personal truth. By living our truth, we stay in alignment. Since our greatest power lies in teaching our children by example and by vibration, I knew my kids would benefit greatly by experiencing their mother being true to herself. Being in alignment is the greatest gift you can give your children. Only by being in alignment are you truly of value to others.

Throughout my marriage to their father, our kids lived a normal life of fun, friends, and good times with the family. The flaw was in their parents' relationship. Toward the end of the marriage, the kids were living in a home where their parents were no longer in love—not an ideal situation. Children need to see and experience parents who deeply care for each other so that they, too, can learn how to be in a loving relationship later in life.

Divorce is hard enough without throwing a third party into the mix. Such was the case when I met the man who would become, in four years' time, my children's stepfather. Here's how it happened.

The children's father, Mark, had booked an African hunting safari and had his heart set on my going, but I never wanted to go to Africa. I love to travel and adore adventure, but something deep down inside of me felt terrified about going to Africa. So, for months I refused to even consider it. I didn't know why, but all I could think about were my initial feelings of fear and apprehension. So deep was my conviction that when the professional guide who was to be our personal guide traveled to our city to meet us, I manifested a cold and didn't attend the meeting. "I'm not going to Africa," I declared, yet again.

But Mark was relentless. "Please go," he pleaded. "Africa is life-changing. It will change your life forever." How prophetic those words would turn out to be. "Please come with me," he said again and again. I don't know if it was his tone of voice or a deep knowing coming to the surface, but something inside of me clicked after many months of refusing. I finally said I would go with him to Africa. Still, I felt apprehensive.

When our plane touched down in Arusha, Tanzania, I looked out my window to the runway below and saw what appeared to be a fuzzy beige jackrabbit hopping past the wheel of our giant 747 airliner. At that moment, which I can only describe as a divine inspiration, I knew to my core that everything was going to be fine. I reached over, smacked Mark on the arm, and declared as much. He looked at me with a shocked expression and seemed pleased that I had finally reached such a conclusion.

Inside, the airport was pandemonium. I was left standing in the midst of it all while Mark went to retrieve our bags from the conveyor belt on the other side of the room. Suddenly, out of nowhere appeared a tallish handsome man with a mustache and silver blonde hair, several years my senior. He was dressed in short shorts and safari garb. I felt my breath catch in my throat as I looked into his bright blue eyes. "You must be Sharon," he said in an amazingly deep voice as he gazed at me. "Indeed I am," I replied, still marveling at how he had magically appeared before me. He introduced himself as our professional hunter, Jay, our guide on this safari. Hmm, indeed.

Over the next fourteen days, I fell in love with this man. From the moment of our first meeting, I felt that I knew him at a deep soul level. It was a profound recognition, and I didn't want to leave his side. He touched the deepest part of me. When I looked into his eyes, I felt I was home. We spent the entire safari in hysterical laughter over nothing in particular, and yet every moment we were together I knew I was following my heart. Where to, I had no idea. In spite of my feelings for him, I allowed myself only thoughts of a deep and mentoring friendship between us. At the time, I never imagined that I would alter my entire life in order to be with him, and that four years after this safari we would marry one another.

The process of deciding what to do with the rest of my life took me almost three years. During this time, I was in a relationship with this new man and felt that he was the love of my life, but I was still convinced that I was supposed to be with my children's father forever. During this period, I continued my long-standing spiritual studies in hope of finding answers, and I prayed a lot.

I remember the day that I started the seed of thought that would grow into a new path. I was visiting a favorite retreat center where I was immersed in daily exercise and spiritual and metaphysical classes. While in my usual relaxed state of asking for internal guidance, a very clear thought came to me: *Maybe you won't be with the children's father forever.* "What?!" I exclaimed, feeling sure that I had yelled it out loud for everyone to hear. I was mortified. The thought went against my belief that Mark and I were destined to stay married.

Once my Internal Guidance System delivered that clear thought to me—*maybe you won't be with the children's father forever*—I felt deep down I had no choice but to consider it. Again, it felt like a small seed inside of me, waiting to grow.

As this process progressed, I received so much help from the Universe. Always paying attention to my heart, what propelled me forward was my Internal Guidance System, listening for messages that were repeated to me over and over and that felt good and right for me. "To thine own self be true" came into my experience that entire year through an array of amazing experiences and remains a poignant example of my IGS at its peak.

At the time, I had a girlfriend who was very in-tune psychically. I had not told her of my involvement with this new man I loved, yet one day she called me and said an intuitive message had come to her. Although she had no idea what it could mean for me, she knew for a fact that it applied to me. "To thine own self be true" was all she said. I almost fell off my chair. During the rest of that year of intense process, this particular message would appear to me in a myriad of ways, dozens of times. I love the magic of the Universe.

This became a time for taking each thought, potential decision, and choice before me to my deepest feeling place. How did I feel about each choice as I thought about it? How did I feel about each of these men—my husband, Mark, and this new man, Jay—as I considered and envisioned my life with each of them? Did it feel right or not right? Could I face life without Jay and go back to Mark on an emotional level? I knew I could only make a correct decision for myself by feeling my way there, by following my Internal Guidance System.

Three years after stepping off that plane in Africa, I awoke to a beautiful fall day at home. And as I awoke, I simply and completely *knew.* I knew to the bottom of my heart, to the core of my soul the answer to my question: I belonged with Jay. I was clear about my future, and I experienced that clarity in a way I never had before.

My years of doubting and searching for answers had come to an end. I would leave my marriage and be with Jay because I felt there was no other choice in my heart and soul. It was an absolute knowing. I have had this level of knowing before in my life, and it is extremely powerful. Such knowing allows all of us to move toward whatever calling, whatever desire, we possess. It allows us to be free of doubts and fear and to know for certain that what we move toward is correct and right for us.

From that moment of intense knowing, I stopped doubting and never looked back. Jay and I have now been married for fifteen happy years.

MY PROCESS, MY VISION

My children's father was devastated by my choice to leave him, and he was sure his life was now a black void. Mark was certain that none of us would ever be happy. On the other hand, once I reached the decision that this was the right thing to do, I knew that all would be well and that everyone in our family would, *in time*, be happy. It was a knowing deep inside me that couldn't be swayed, and within this knowing I held the highest vision for my children's lives, for my own life, and also their father's. This vision encompassed everyone's wellbeing and happiness and foretold all of us living our best life.

Their father did not share my vision. When I told him that we would all be friends one day and share holidays together, he told me I was crazy. Still, I held my vision. I didn't participate in his anger. I knew this would all work out.

It's important to mention that to *hope* for something is not enough to sway the Universe and manifest it. You must *know* that the vision of what you want is already ensured. By knowing that something is already yours, and then allowing it to be so, it will manifest. This is a formidable power that comes from a very clear place of absolute knowing.

This isn't to say that the transition was easy for my children. I'll never forget telling them that their parents were divorcing. It was one of the worst days I have ever experienced. I saw their heartbreak and felt it as my own. Still, I knew I had to do this. There was a power and force inside of me that said, "No choice." So strong was this desire that I truly felt I had no alternative but to unravel our family unit and create a new one, which certainly wouldn't be easy. The children were resentful and unwilling, which was clearly understandable. I was leaving their father for another man, and they were not happy with my choice. I knew they must be allowed their process, which would involve adjusting to two family households and healing the hurt they felt.

I had chosen a man who was substantially different from my children's father. It would be hard for them to adjust to having Jay in their lives, but I wanted them to know that there were many types of parents, as well as many ways to parent. I also wanted them to experience me living my own truth. Most of all, I wanted them to experience parents who were in a loving and healthy relationship.

I did my best to discuss these issues with the kids. Given their young ages, they weren't very receptive to my reasons, so I explained things gradually. I knew that in time, their own life experience would show them that I had made the right choice. How they felt each day would determine the level of participation and acceptance they were ready for. I wanted them to be close to Jay, but only they could determine the pace at which they would get to know him. This would be determined by how they felt and what degree of closeness they wanted. I knew I couldn't force it, and at times it felt painfully slow. The only way to ensure a happy outcome would be to allow them the time they needed.

By not pressuring them to feel any certain way, my kids could closely and accurately listen to their own IGS. At first I could sense that their Internal Guidance Systems were telling them the divorce and having a stepfather were not good things. It was often strained and uncomfortable when the kids came back home from visiting their dad, as they had not yet accepted Jay. I completely believed that the children would come to feel differently once they had experienced more time with our new family dynamic, felt the love between us and the love we had for them. As the years passed, the children came to see and feel the true essence of Jay. The time he devoted to them, his loving and helpful ways, and his endless patience showed the kids how much he truly loved them, and they in turn came to love him dearly.

Mark was angry with me for about two years following the divorce, but he continued to be civil to me and lovingly raise our three children. He willingly helped create a parenting schedule that worked for us both. He soon remarried, as well, which meant that his new wife became my children's stepmother—another adjustment for the kids.

The process of adjusting to their parents' divorce and adapting to their new stepparents was difficult and challenging for my children, but my vision did come true. Our two households have shared many happy holidays and birthdays together, and the children eventually found great value in having two sets of parents who love them. We have all done our best to ensure that the children's lives are happy and emotionally healthy.

The children learned that staying connected to their feelings is an important aspect of adapting and healing. Being aware of how they are feeling and allowing their actions to support their feelings makes them more able to accurately follow their IGS. Their own experience helped them to understand, accept, and ultimately support the changes I made in our lives using my own Internal Guidance System.

THE CHALLENGE OF STEPPARENTS

Try telling your young children that the negative situations and people in their lives are their greatest teachers, and you may discover that they don't receive this news well at all. Children seldom see the big picture, only what is in their immediate reality. Learning from adversity is not something they are naturally attuned to. Rather, when something or someone unwanted is in their life, they may think of that thing or person as bad, even hateful, as opposed to a learning moment.

The concept of life lessons—using a difficult or unpleasant experience to come to a new understanding about yourself and others—needs to be sensitively approached with younger kids. Depending on their age and their feelings about the particular situation, you'll need to explain this concept many times over the course of their childhood for it to be fully integrated. But your words won't be their only teachers; what your child experiences will demonstrate the truths they need to learn.

Adapting to their stepmother was a challenging yet valuable learning experience for my kids. She came into their lives when Dustin was about five, Raven was eight, and Brittany was eleven. Over the years, it was Dustin whom I encouraged and coached the most with regard to his stepmom. Maybe this was because I had his undivided attention on our long drives home from school, and he was the child who seemed to have the most trouble making things work with her.

Initially, my support involved giving Dustin reassurance more than anything else—helping him know that he was loved by both of his parental households and that everyone had his best interests at heart. As he got a little older, had more life experience, and could more easily understand the philosophy of the Universal Law of Attraction, I shared with him what I had learned about relating to people. One of the concepts involved not being attached to eliciting a certain result or response from another person. This related to what was going on between him and his stepmom. Their interactions were often confusing to him, and he reacted by pushing against the situation and getting angry.

I wanted Dustin to understand that our relationships, whether with our parents, stepparents, siblings, friends, or teachers, help us to grow. They also help us decide who we want to be and what we want to experience in any given situation. Very often we have to experience what we *don't* want to find out what we *do* want. Dustin's experience of unclear communication between him and his stepmom taught him that in order to have a chance at getting what he wanted, he needed to be clear about his wishes. He also came to understand that **he has no control over how others receive his way of communicating.**

By arguing with her, Dustin was pushing so hard against what he didn't want that the Universe was pushing back by blocking any chance that they would be able to hear and understand each other. I explained to Dustin that when you push against what you don't want, you not only don't get what you want—you also feel frustrated and filled with negative feelings.

One reason that relationships provide a teaching opportunity is that they offer a mirror in which to examine our own qualities. **What we love or despise in others mirrors those parts of**

ourselves that we also love or despise. If we're paying attention, we will see the parts of ourselves that we love and also the parts we keep hidden. These are aspects of ourselves we don't want to acknowledge and often don't even know are present. It is then that we can choose to let go of or change the parts of ourselves that don't serve us. Our relationships, whether with a chosen friend or a relative whom we haven't chosen, help us learn how to deal with the ebb and flow of our lives. All relationships require give and take, as well as compromise at times. The nature of most children is to be reactive to others. They may spend a lot of time feeling bad when they can't control events or people—which is nearly all the time, as we can't control others. But what they can do, and what you can gently encourage them to do, is to manage their experience by choosing their actions and not pushing against people and situations.

We have no control over others—not our divorcing parents, our stepparents, or anyone else—but we can learn to choose our reactions. And when we get really good at it, we will find that we are actually going with the flow ... a true art.

WORDS OF WISDOM FOR DIVORCING PARENTS AND CHILDREN OF DIVORCE

Everyone's divorce is different. Circumstances and personalities differ, as does the time it takes for ex-spouses and children to adjust to a new life. Children of divorce, however, tend to have a similar response to their parents splitting up; they are generally upset, angry, anxious, and sad. Most kids, regardless of their age and their parents' situation, want their mom and dad to stay together. And it's rarely easy to adjust to stepparents and new family dynamics. Both parents and children can acknowledge these truths while also respecting the wisdom of the Universal Law of Attraction and their Internal

Guidance Systems. Here are some helpful guidelines for parents and children who are going through the changes brought on by divorce.

For divorcing parents:

- Ask yourself: Are you choosing your path consciously? How do you feel about the choice you are making?

- Have no guilt and no regrets. Live your truth, come from a place of love, and you will not make a mistake.

- Your soul wants to express who you really are. The choices of your spirit—what your soul wants—will always be for your highest good.

- You are in tune with your Source when you are in alignment, feeling positive emotion and joy. Use every opportunity to create your wellbeing.

For children of divorce:

- Everything that you experience creates who you really are. Value those experiences and the people who help you experience new things. Know that not all people or experiences will result in good feelings, but they will result in new insights about yourself and life in general.

- Everything that appears negative has a gift within it. Have faith and allow it to become apparent.

- What you decide about an experience is what you will experience.

- If something isn't going the way you wanted or envisioned, be patient with yourself and those involved.

Dealing with your child's range of emotions surrounding your divorce can be tricky. Our number one rule as parents should always be to love our children, which is the greatest gift we can give them. But there are also some practical guidelines we can follow. These suggestions for divorcing parents are adapted from the Mayo Clinic website.[2]

- "It's best if you and your spouse can tell your child about the divorce together. Speak honestly and simply, and skip the ugly details."

- "Remind your child—repeatedly if necessary—that he or she did nothing to cause the divorce and that both of you love your child as much as ever."

- "As you work out the terms of the divorce, try to maintain your child's routine as much as possible—or be quick to establish a new routine. Knowing what to expect will help your child feel more secure."

- "Encourage your child to share his or her feelings as openly as possible."

- "Don't speak badly about your spouse in front of your child; don't make accusations against your spouse in front of your child; don't force your child to choose sides; and don't use your child as a messenger or go-between."

- "Help your child maintain a strong, loving relationship with the other parent as you work toward meeting common parenting goals."

---

[2]   http://www.mayoclinic.com/health/divorce/HO00055

NOTES

CHAPTER 9

Inspiring Your Children

D o you work to inspire your children rather than trying to change them? When we inspire rather than try to manage our kids, our relationship to them is more respectful and less fraught with conflict. And the influence we have is also more effective. Why? Because when we inspire our children, we tap into a deeper, more spiritual place within them and within ourselves.

As I have emphasized throughout the book, being an example to your children—a role model who embodies your most deeply held values—and sending out your highest vibration are the most important teaching tools you can provide. I shared with you how my father inspired me with his passion for life, his joyful outlook, and his resilience in the face of tough obstacles. I am so grateful for the lessons he provided just by being his truest self. I was inspired by his actions more than his words because, as we all know, children tend to watch how we behave more than they listen to what we say.

In this final chapter, I want to inspire you to be your highest inspiration to your children so that they can become the uniquely wonderful individuals they were meant to be. By following your own Internal Guidance System and encouraging your kids to follow theirs, your influence will indeed be inspirational.

INSPIRATION THROUGH VIBRATION

In chapter two, we talked about how our energy vibration influences everyone around us. And of course this is certainly true with our children. In review, the Universe responds to our vibration, which is what we emit with our thoughts and feelings, and sends what matches it back to us in our manifestations. Our children respond to our vibration and behave in the manner that's consistent with how we're feeling. In other words, what we send out to our children— our energy—touches them deeply and influences them profoundly. When we hold the highest vision of them via our thoughts, beliefs, and expectations, our children can't help but be influenced and inspired to rise to that vibration.

Inspiring our kids also involves showing them that we respect their developmental process, that we honor the various paths they may choose as they become who they are, and that we appreciate their individuality. Our children give us the experience of themselves based on what we expect from or believe about them. This is simply the Law of Attraction at work. We will always receive what we expect and believe. So let's expect our kids to be themselves, the best expression of who they are, and believe in their ability to become their own unique person and create the life they want.

I suggest that all of us who are parents engage in this simple process as often as we can:

- Hold a vision of your child as who he or she really is, their highest self.

- Whenever you think about your child or are with them face-to-face, focus on this highest vision of them.

- Practice this thought: *My child is in the process of becoming who she/he was meant to be, creating the life she/he came to create.*

When you engage in this process, the vision of your child as their highest self will become dominant in your thoughts over time. This means it will become what you believe. Once it's dominant and you are able to maintain this focus regarding your child, you'll discover that they will reflect that vision, meaning that is how you'll experience them.

We can tell our children that we love them, but it's even more important that they *feel* our love on an energetic level. Our energy vibration is the powerful place of our higher selves, of the Universe. And children are more profoundly affected by what they feel—the vibration they receive in any given experience—than by anything else. This is why it's important to be in alignment as much of the time as you can in relation to your kids. When you are with them, see the best and expect the best from them. Be sure your thoughts match your actions and desires for your child. **Again, your vibration is more powerful than anything you can say or do.** By feeling good and making the decision to foster your inner joy and calm, you will inspire your children with your support and your love on every level.

Regardless of their age, children know when you are merely *acting* lovingly but aren't *feeling* loving. In this sense, children are wonderful teachers and truly can keep us accountable. On some level, they recognize when we are not in alignment.

There have definitely been times in my own life when my kids saw through my "act" and called me on it. So when I felt the discrepancy between my actions and my vibration, I would leave the room for a few minutes to get back to feeling good as much as possible. This way I would have a more authentic influence on my children, and they wouldn't feel the dissonance in my energetic vibration.

The bottom line is this: children need to feel your love on a vibrational level—deep and personal. And to do this, you need to be in alignment. So let's review what that means.

ALIGNMENT = LOVING VIBRATION

What does it mean to be in alignment? It means you are offering one vibration (one signal) to the Universe: simply, that you feel good. When you're in alignment, you have a desire that you believe you can manifest and you don't have doubts or feel negatively about this desire. You're thinking your most positive thoughts, the same thoughts as your Source (or higher self). The result is that your thoughts, desires, and emotions are aligned into one true signal. Your energy isn't split with contradicting thoughts, and you feel great.

Your children can't feel your love when you're out of alignment. The highest vibration in the Universe is your love. It is one pure, ideal vibration.

When you feel bad, the energy you send toward your child generally includes whatever negative feelings or thoughts you're having in the moment. Perhaps these thoughts are triggered by disrespectful behavior or poor performance in school. There are countless scenarios that can cause parents to feel unfavorably toward their children. More than likely, your energy expresses disapproval of your child, which makes it very challenging for them to feel your love. On the energetic level, your child will not feel the pure power of your love and support when you send out a contradictory vibration along with it. Sending contradictory vibrations means that you are out of alignment, and when you are out of alignment, you can't be the inspiration for your child that you want to be. **Your power and**

influence, your ability to inspire your child to become his or her highest self, rest in your being in alignment.

Remember: Your *feelings* are your guidance system. When you feel good, you are in alignment with your higher self. When you feel negative emotion, you are out of alignment.

So how do you make sure that you are in alignment when confronting a parenting challenge? Let's say your thirteen-year-old daughter comes to you and says she wants to get her tongue pierced. The idea makes you cringe, but you want to encourage her to use her own IGS—and you also want to be in sync with your own highest self. Your objective is to be in alignment as you gently guide her toward making the decision that will allow her to feel in alignment with her highest self.

The notion of a tongue piercing may initially cause you to be out of alignment, feeling anger, disappointment, or fear. Before you open your mouth and tell your daughter any thoughts on the matter, you first want to make sure you feel better. You can do this in a number of ways. Perhaps just remembering that a stud in your child's tongue is not the end of the world and that there are far worse choices she could make will set your mind at ease. Or you may need to remove yourself from the situation for a while and do something that makes you feel good.

Next, you want to make sure that your child has the awareness of being in alignment with her choices, as opposed to acting impulsively and without regard for her own feelings. You might ask her these powerful questions, which will allow her to check in with her feelings:

- How do you feel about making this choice?
- Do you feel that this choice reflects who you are?

- How do you feel this choice enhances you?
- Is this something you really want or something your friends want you to do?

Again, you want to encourage your child to make her choices when she feels good and creating her highest choice, as opposed to following someone else's lead and having any doubts whatsoever.

INSPIRATION, MOM-ISMS, AND TATTOOS

When I asked my adult daughters, who are now in their twenties, to write something for this book based on their experiences growing up with a mom who tried to inspire them to follow the Universal Law of Attraction and their Internal Guidance Systems, they generously agreed, remembering all the positive times and also the very challenging times. And they didn't hold back from telling it like it was—and is—from their unique perspectives. So here is Brittany's take on a mom's influence. Raven's follows.

In Brittany's Words ...

Everyone has "Mom-isms" that they carry throughout their life, guiding them usually in spite of themselves. These are usually kept to oneself, partly because no one else could possibly understand, but most importantly because God forbid Mom had been right all those years. The Mom-isms I carry with me haunt my every waking moment, and not only are they specific to our family, but they resonate in the lives of other people who actually pay her good money to also hear her voice in the back of their head.

In all seriousness, my mother is the guiding light in my life. This is somewhat of a given because she is, after all, my mother. But, she is a special kind of mother. There is an allotted amount of her driving me crazy (which is very reciprocal), but the great part is that every single thing she does comes from a place of love. I have been fortunate in many ways, and what I've come to realize more and more over the years is how accepting and supportive my mom is. This has been a process that has been ever-developing and is now more prevalent than ever.

Being her daughter, as well as her being our mother, has been an ongoing evolution. Truthfully, I wouldn't go back and change too much of it.

My mother has taught me, first and foremost, that there is nothing more important than that I feel good today. Nobody and nothing is worth sacrificing my feeling happy. We are here on this Earth to have fun and live our best life. We are here to create, and we cannot create our highest path if it does not come from a place of feeling good. It's just that simple, and just that complicated.

Feeling good sounds good, right? Well, until someone runs over your dog or your boyfriend breaks up with you. These, along with a long list of other things, are facts of life, and they are things that are going to happen. But it's what you choose to do when these events occur that either make it worse, or make you better.

Through the ups and downs of my life, I have learned to let go of expectation and just trust. I've also learned how much the little things really do matter in affecting the bigger picture. In fact, they may be the only things that really do matter.

When something isn't going our way, we want to fix it. We want to immediately go to the heart of the issue and just fix whatever is wrong, but this isn't always possible. In fact, rarely is it at all possible, and this was a hard thing for me to accept regarding a certain relationship. I always wanted to have the difficult conversation, push the matter, which eventually leads to it pushing back just as hard—which is another key factor: what you resist persists. It's simply the Law of Attraction. What you push against is going to push back with an opposite and equal amount of force. The truth is, we can't fix everything, and if we can, it's probably not going to be in the timeline or the way we imagine it being anyway.

So, the key is to let it go, which, by no accident, is the hardest thing to do. Letting go is something we struggle with our whole lives, but it's really the only way to live. You have to know that everything is perfect, and it will only happen for your highest good. The key is staying in a good-feeling place. Now to my point: how do we get there? Naturally, we want to get there by fixing the problem. We've been over this … it's not always possible. But, the beauty of the good-feeling place is that it doesn't have to have anything to do with the issue at hand. In fact, it's sometimes better if it doesn't. What makes you feel good? Who makes you feel good? Maybe it's watching that stupid YouTube video of that kid waking up from anesthetics after a dental appointment. Maybe going to your best friend's house and painting your nails makes you feel good, or watching that movie that makes you roll over and laugh until your side hurts. It is that simple. Stay feeling good. Your good-feeling place doesn't know the difference; it just knows that it feels good.

This may be the number one most important thing that I've taken away from my mother's teachings. It's the root of everything, the foundation. I even have a notecard on my mirror, decorated in bright colors, that says, "There is nothing more important than that I feel good today." It takes practice, and it's a constant, conscious process that will never end. We're always going to run into things that challenge our happiness and make it difficult, but every time we bounce back, we come up a little bit higher than the last time.

My mother is my angel and my best friend, and I wouldn't know any of these things without her, nor would I be anywhere near where I am today, which is a pretty darn good place. I don't know how to say that without sounding cliché, but clichés are there because they're true.

As for the dog and the boyfriend: you loved that dog and it loved you back, and that is all we're here to do, is to love. And the boyfriend? The right one will stick, I promise you that. Thanks, Mom.

In Raven's words …

I haven't always been the easiest daughter to live with. I worked really hard at making my high school career as difficult on everyone as possible. While this looked different for each family member, there was more or less an equal sense of unpleasantness experienced by each of my four parents. I have never felt anything less than unconditionally loved, but I tested the definition of unconditional.

I found everything to fight about and managed to get caught for any and all broken rules. All the screaming, silent treatments, punishments, and general unrest aside, my mother has turned out to be one of my very best friends.

My mom has been sharing, educating, and enforcing her knowledge about the Universe, God, angels, my own IGS, energy, and overall healthy living for as long as I can remember. She has always tried to provide us (me and my siblings) with the tools to succeed. By succeed, I mean first and foremost to be happy and attract positivity. In congruence with these goals, she taught us to choose a mindset that allows us to achieve the things we want in this life. I don't get through the day without employing the tools Mom has given me to maintain my happiness while deliberately creating my life.

As a family unit, we are normal in all the right ways and abnormal in even better ways. I am indescribably thankful for my mom's life guidance. The tools she has armed me with have assisted in malfunctions of every type: heartbreak, physical health, positive manifestation, and creating what I want.

In high school, I was in a constant place of defiance and nonconformity. Reasonably, this translated into fighting, overall unpleasantness, and an ongoing tension between my mom and me. At sixteen, I decided a needed a break. So, naturally, I ran away. As far as I can remember, I did so without expectation or forethought at all. But what I do remember is that I didn't see any other way to handle myself. What transcended that experience was the way in which my mother received me upon my return. There was no spite or anger as a response to my selfish choices. She welcomed me home, letting go of the terror I put her and my dad through. She had the capacity to react in this way because of her belief system and faith in my own adherence to the tools she had helped to instill in me. Her understanding of the Universe and dedication to maintaining joy and happiness in her life, and ours, makes all things possible.

I wasn't always thrilled with my mom's parental interjections, and to this day we disagree on her level of strictness, but what we do agree on is that neither of us would take each other any other way. Although I was pretty convinced then that she was joyfully creating Hell on earth for me, I somehow survived. I am thankful for the person that she is, which in turn has helped me decide the person that I want to be.

On a basic level, it is easy enough to understand that all thoughts, actions, and intentions have a vibration, and based on what you are feeling (and projecting) you will receive its match in what you manifest. Before I truly understood the workings of the Universe, there were times when I didn't feel like I deserved to attract some of the things I got. For example, in the last year or so, I have had multiple unwanted incidences with my car—two break-ins and a hit-and-run. In keeping with my mom's teachings, while none of these things were directly or physically my doing, I had attracted them. I was a match to these occurrences.

It can be hard to figure out the reason negative things happen to you. I love and appreciate my car every day. I even call her by name. I take good care of her, attempting to ensure her safety and wellbeing. How am I a vibrational match to these car troubles?

What I do know is this: A continued appreciation of all things and an attitude of positive expectation, not only toward my car but (evidently) also in all the aspects of my life, will maintain the prosperity of my belongings and my Self.

I do know that the laws of the Universe are absolute. Like any faith, faith in the Law of Attraction requires awareness and practice. My mom explains that this law is constant and ever-present, whether you believe in it or not. What you can do is work with it and use it to create the life that you want.

I struggle to create a picture that does justice to my mom's influence on the person that I am today. Her teachings on the Law of Attraction and following my own IGS have immensely heightened my quality of life. I know that I ultimately have control over the outcome of my life and everything that happens within it. I am in complete control of what I experience, all of the wanted and unwanted things. I take responsibility for my life.

One of the most important singular ideas that my mom has ever taught me is "choose joy." When everything else gets muddy and unclear, and when the right choice is disguised and complex, just get back to this one concise statement: choose joy. In fact, to insure that I never lose sight of it, I recently had this "Mom-ism" permanently tattooed on my left forearm in my own mother's handwriting. Now, even if I tried my very hardest to forget or deny this idea, I cannot. My mom says it best: "We just like to be happy."

We heard from Dustin in chapter four, but I don't want to leave him out of this final chapter. Here are some summary thoughts my eighteen-year-old son had about how I've tried to inspire him.

In Dustin's words ...

Throughout my whole life, there has been a little voice in the back of my head guiding me through the toughest of situations. I like to call this voice my mother. My mom has been a massive influence on the person I have become, and especially on the happiness I experience. She taught me about happiness and how so many people live such a low quality of life struggling to find it. The truth is, it's not something that needs to be found because it's right there within you. Everything that one feels is manifested within you, and if we can be taught to look inside ourselves, the possibilities are endless. My mother is living proof of this.

I am so proud of my mom and how far she has come since she discovered this hidden truth. She has passed it on to me, and now it is your turn to pass it on to others.

LOVING UNCONDITIONALLY, LIVING YOUR TRUTH

As I complete this book, my children are all young adults. I feel a sense of accomplishment that is truly blissful. Not because they are, or were, the perfect kids, but because they are happy, functional, loving people whom I have sent out into the world. They have learned to follow their own IGS, which is continuing to lead them to their best lives. They are empowered beings who will follow the beat of their own drum, always.

I have said to each of my children that I am here to lend support in any way they want me to, and I've encouraged them to never ask me what they should do or what choices they should make. I have taught them that those answers are within themselves. I will always support whichever path they choose, but they must choose it and create it.

I did not start out being the ideal parent I wanted to be. I had to learn by doing—and often by doing things the "wrong way." I tried to control the uncontrollable, failing to consult with my IGS and forgetting that my children needed to find their own paths for themselves.

After many years of trial and error and becoming more deeply involved in the Law of Attraction, I have created my ideal relationship with each of my children. I believe they know who they are in relation to me. I believe they feel safe with me because I don't judge or criticize them. They don't feel defensive, because a child who grows up free from criticism has no need to be defensive. On the other hand, I can say bold things to them and make them accountable by asking them an appropriate question at the right time. We laugh easily and often, and we laugh at everything. My children have always brought out the kid in me, and at times I can be the silliest one in our group. That is my idea of experiencing my highest joy.

So I encourage you to teach your children to be inspired by God and to know that the Universe is on their side in creating their highest self. Inspire them to express their joy, share their loving smiles, dance their dance, and celebrate their miraculous spirit!

In closing, I'd like to leave you with these inspiring words.

Remind yourself:

- When you love your children unconditionally, they learn to love themselves and others in this way.

- Appreciation and thankfulness are the most powerful statements to the Universe. As you appreciate the small and large details of your life and the world around you, you will receive more things to appreciate.

- There is nothing more important than to feel good.

- What you focus on expands, moves toward you, and becomes your manifestation.

- Be non-judgmental of your children and yourself.

- Listen for your truth through your heart (IGS).

- Clarify your desires —what you want—by experiencing what you *don't* want.

- Inspire others to rise to your high-energy vibration.

- Pay attention to your thoughts. Refocus when a thought doesn't feel good.

- Observe the behavior of your children and choose how you will respond. Don't participate in the drama.

- Respect your child's individual life path. Lend support without controlling.

- Teach your children to make their own choices separate from your desires for them.

- Have faith and trust in yourself and in the Universe. Faith and trust bring forth your desires with ease.

- You can do and be whatever you can imagine, so teach your children to know this, too.

- There is no right way or "shoulds" in life, only what you are inspired to create.

- The process of life is your reward. No failure is possible because you are always moving forward.

- What you share and give comes back to you. Ask, as there is an abundance of everything you want in the Universe.

- You are one with God and all that exists.

- To love is the greatest gift you can give.

Remind your children:

- What you *know* in your heart and feel so intensely that no one can dissuade you from it transcends people's opinions, known facts, and often even logic. What you feel inside and believe without doubt—that is your truth.

- There is no right or wrong in your life; there is only what moves you *toward* what you want and what moves you *away* from what you want. Something serves you if it takes you in the direction of what you want. An action or idea doesn't serve you if it moves you away from where you want to go.

- In every moment of your life, you are in the process of deciding who you are. Life is your process of creation. Have the most fun you can have; reach for your highest dream. The possibilities are endless.

- Rather than judging your experiences and yourself by how others judge you, understand that your own Internal Guidance System will always know *your* personal truth.

- Go after what you want with everything you have and without being attached to particular results. If your happiness depends on a certain result, you'll feel disappointed if you don't receive it. If you trust that the result will always be for your highest good, you can never be disappointed.

- End results aren't always as we envision them, but they will always serve our highest ideal.

- What you *intend* is a very powerful force and a conscious statement to the Universe.

- You have come here to experience yourself and to have a creative experience.

- Honor yourself first. You can only acknowledge the good in others by first finding it within yourself.

- Only you can know your path.

- What you believe and expect will determine your experience and your manifestations.

- Create your own joy. Don't look to others to create it for you.

- Joy and happiness lie within you. You are whole as you are. You need nothing outside of yourself to be happy.

N O T E S

You can find Sharon at www.SharonBallantine.com.

Request a free video from her online Parenting course, "The Ballantine Parenting Institute."™

Printed in the United States
By Bookmasters